— YUMMY —
WATERCOLOR

A Beginner's Guide to Painting Cakes, Cookies, Donuts & Other Sweet Treats with Easy Step-by-Step Instructions

CAMILLE BELLET

BETTER DAY BOOKS®
HAPPY • CREATIVE • CURATED

Originally published as *Aquarelle gourmande.* © First published in French by Mango, Paris, France – 2024.

Translated from the French by Rebecca DeWald

English Edition
Publisher: Peg Couch
Book Designer: Llara Pazdan
Editors: Jules Hostetter and Colleen Dorsey

French Edition
Management: Guillaume Pô
Chief Editor: Tatiana Delesalle
Editing: Barbara Janssens
Art Director: Chloé Eve
Design and Layout: Caroline Soulères
Editorial Operations: Emeline Plessier
Production Manager: Thierry Dubus
Production Operations: Marie Guibert

Library of Congress Control Number: 2025946078

ISBN: 978-0-7643-7070-0
ePub: 978-1-5073-0694-9
Printed in China
10 9 8 7 6 5 4 3 2 1

Published by Better Day Books, an imprint of Schiffer Publishing, Ltd.

MIX
Paper | Supporting responsible forestry
FSC® C104723
FSC www.fsc.org

BETTER DAY BOOKS®

SCHIFFER PUBLISHING

Better Day Books
Email: hello@betterdaybooks.com
Web: www.betterdaybooks.com
Visit us on Instagram!
@better_day_books

Schiffer Publishing
4880 Lower Valley Road
Atglen, PA 19310
Phone: 610-593-1777
Fax: 610-593-2002
Email: info@schifferbooks.com
Web: www.schifferbooks.com

INTRODUCTION

My interests in fashion, art, cooking, and illustration, coupled with my spirituality, have led me to follow my dreams and become who I am today: a happy and fulfilled watercolor artist who specializes in illustrations of sweet treats and baking!

I bring an attitude of curiosity and observation to everything around me, both in my personal life and professional practice, which gives me a certain sensitivity that nourishes my inspiration.

Sketchbooks, museum visits, cultural events, discussions, traveling, nature walks, and Pinterest boards all form parts of my creative inventory. I am a lifelong learner with a thirst for knowledge, so I love to frequently change my style and push myself to get out of my comfort zone.

That ability to see every experience as an adventure to savor is what I would like to pass on to you with this book. It is through living, exploring, and practicing that you will foster your creativity and find inspiration.

The step-by-step guides in this book are meant not only to teach but also to inspire you—interpret them in your own way and experiment to your heart's content. It's up to you to find the approach that is right for you!

"Do whatever brings you to life, then. Follow your own fascinations, obsessions, and compulsions. Trust them. Create whatever causes a revolution in your heart. The rest of it will take care of itself."

Elizabeth Gilbert, *Big Magic*, 2016, p. 101

In other words, do what brings you joy!

Camille

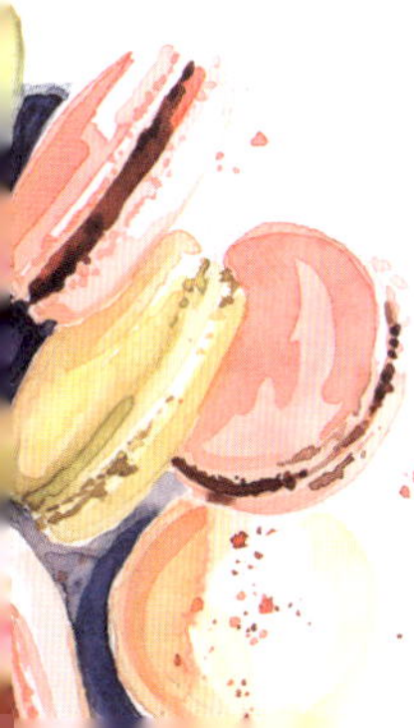

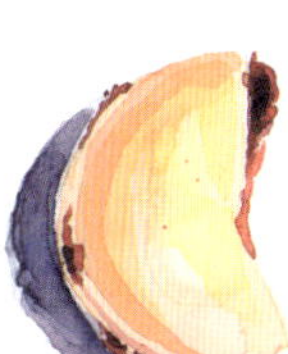

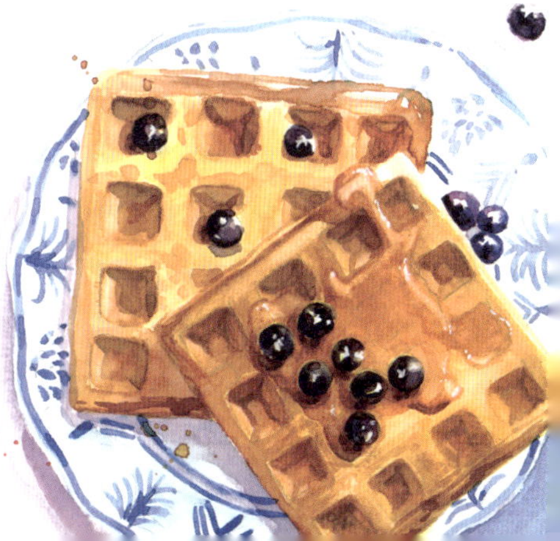

CONTENTS

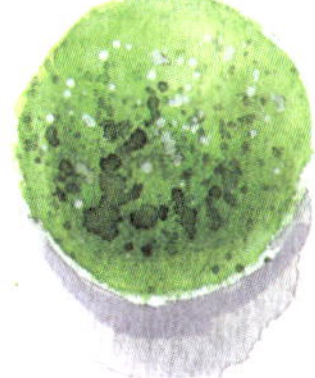

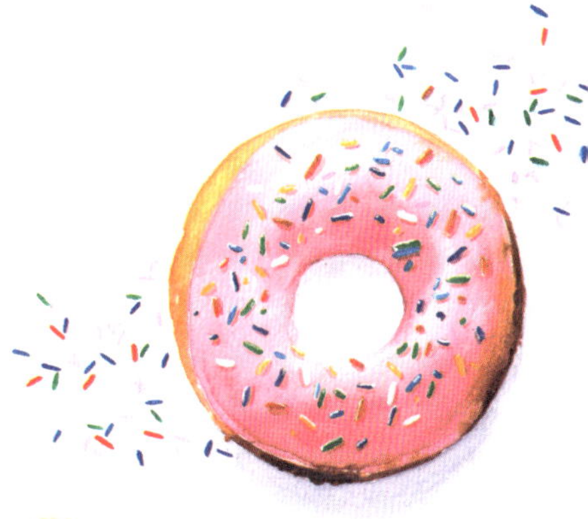

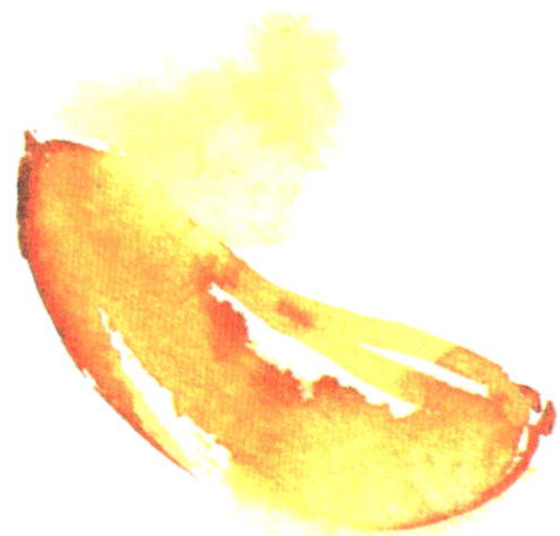

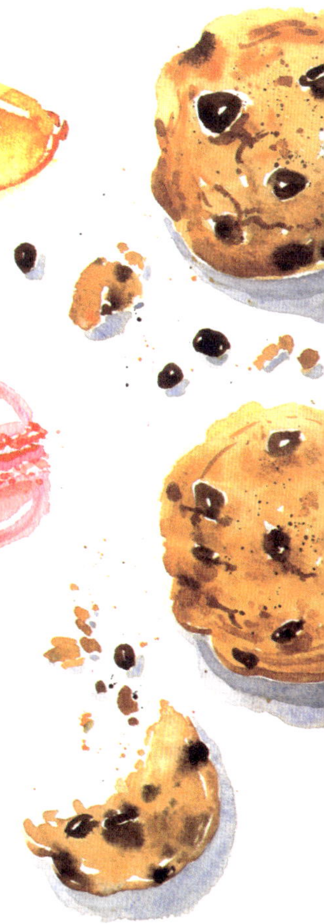

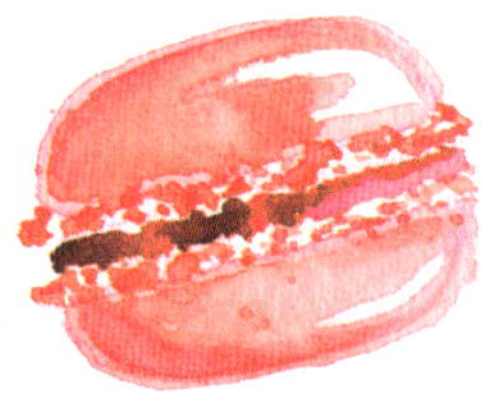

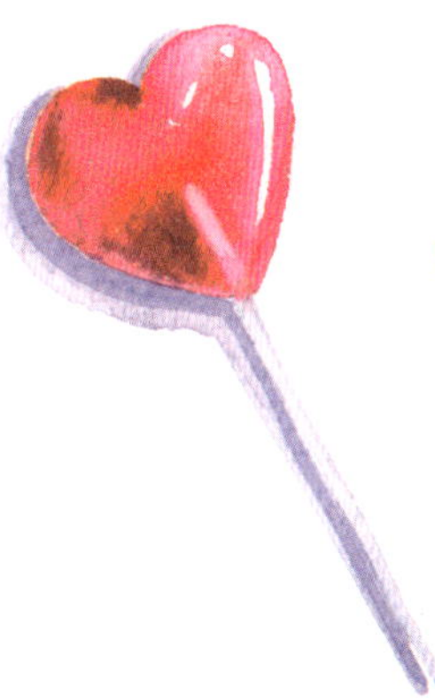

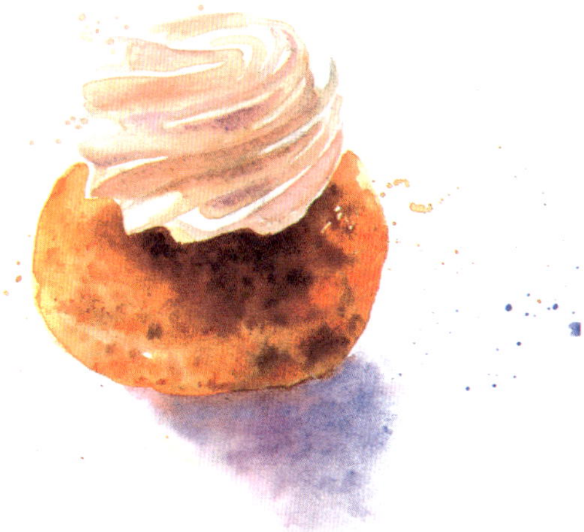

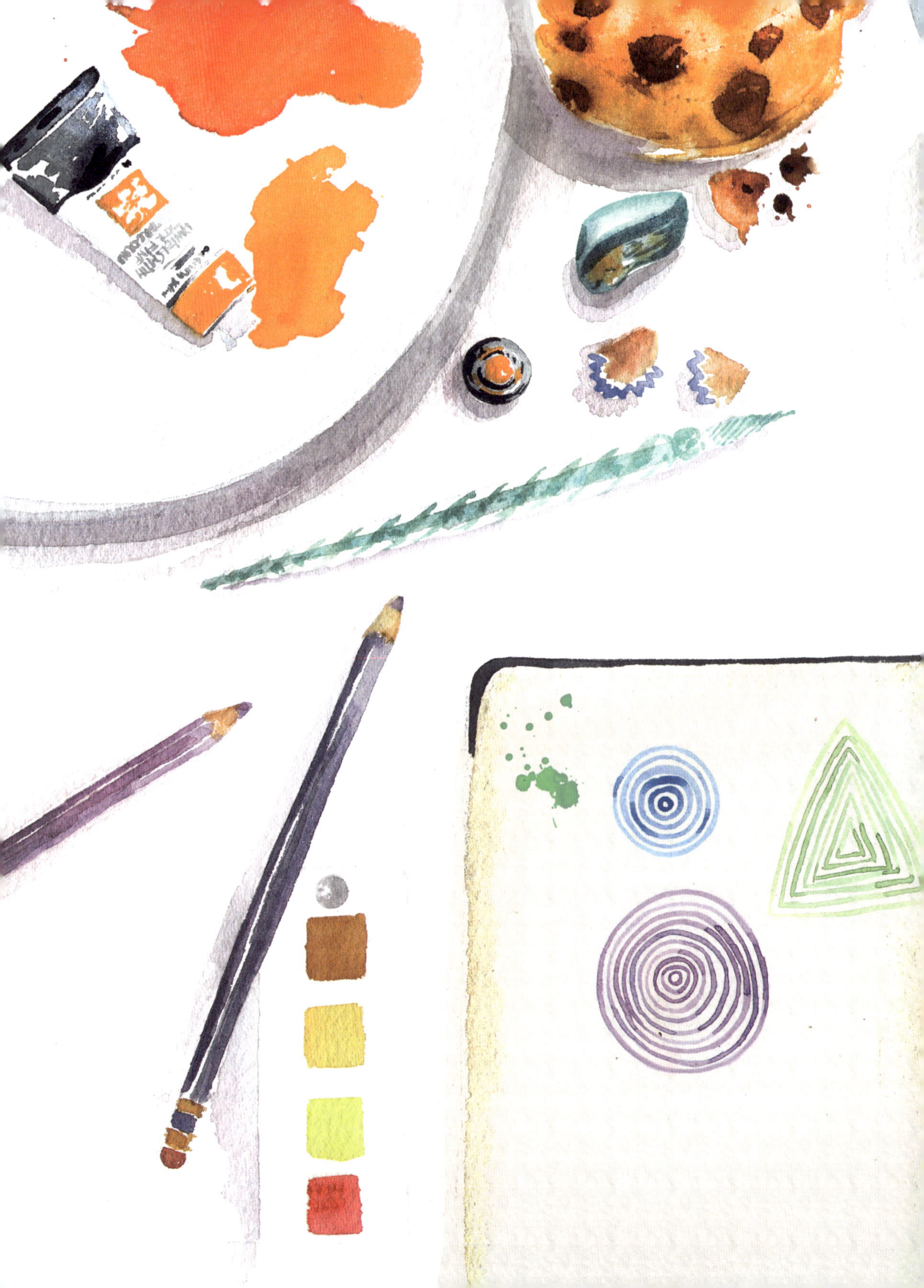

Materials

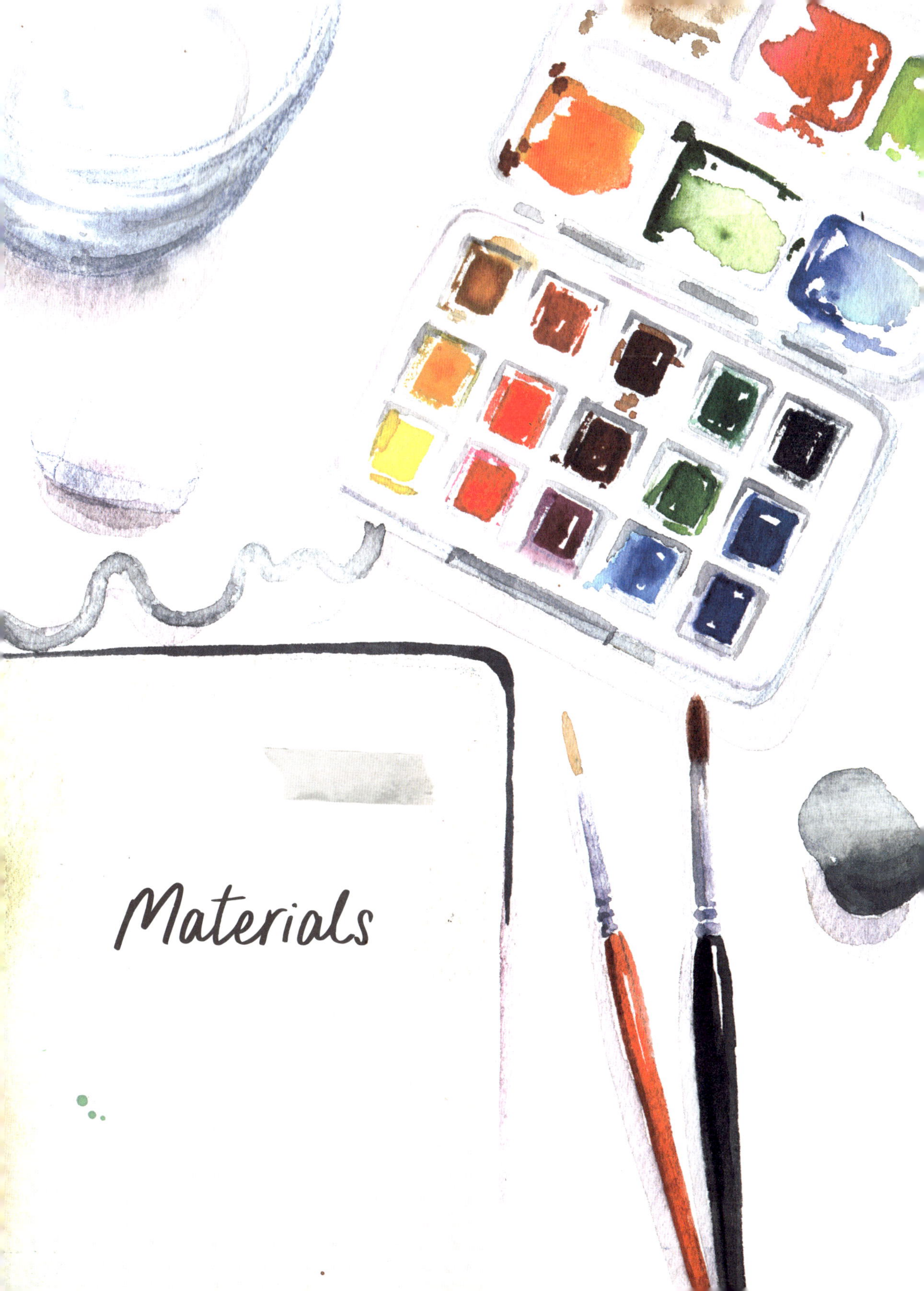

PAINTS

I primarily use 15 colors from the Van Gogh pans range. If you're a beginner, it's best to start by working with just a few colors so that you can develop the skill of blending more-complex colors yourself. Over time, if you find that you enjoy painting with watercolors, you can invest in additional beautiful, ready-to-use paint colors.

I have created designs with somewhat limited palettes for this book to encourage you to create your own color mixtures. You can make your own color charts and keep them handy while painting. Through experimenting and mixing pigments, you will build confidence in your abilities, which is a very important step.

In watercolor painting, you don't really need the colors white or black. To draw attention to light and light areas, you can strategically make use of the blank space on the paper. This creates a more natural and realistic look in your illustrations. Using white pigments in watercolors can make your colors look like gouache, which is a little thicker and less transparent. It's better to learn and use the lifting-off technique to retain blank spaces so that you're picking up good habits from the get-go. You will see in the projects that we won't be using black at all; instead, we'll use Payne's gray, burnt sienna, ultramarine deep, or a deep purple to make a color darker or create shadows.

To paint beautiful, realistic delicacies, you should stick to warm colors. You will also need neutral hues, including shades of brown, gray, and beige. You can either mix these hues from primary colors or buy them ready-made.

Watercolors in tubes are easier to use than watercolors in pans. They are a little more expensive (depending on the brand and size of the tube), but it's worth the investment in the long term, because tubes contain much more paint. You will need only small amounts of paint for any single design, though.

Exercise

Make a color chart of your palette and lay it out on the page in neat rows like the colors in an off-the-shelf palette. This is a very useful exercise when starting out to help you get to know your colors and imagine their combinations!

My Personal Color Palette

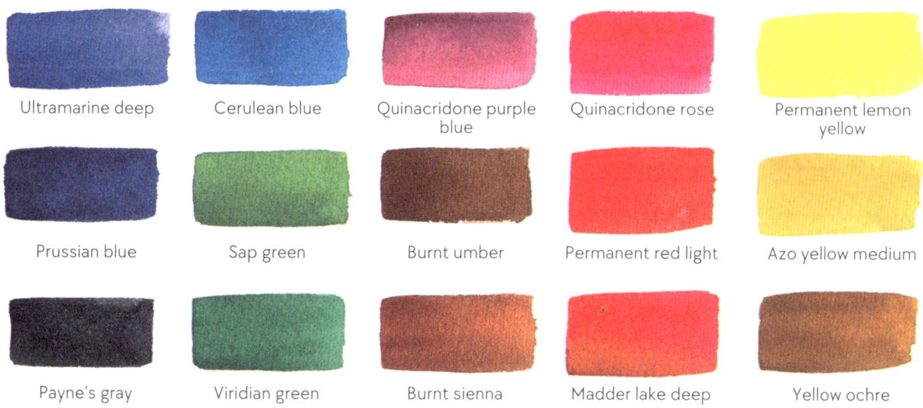

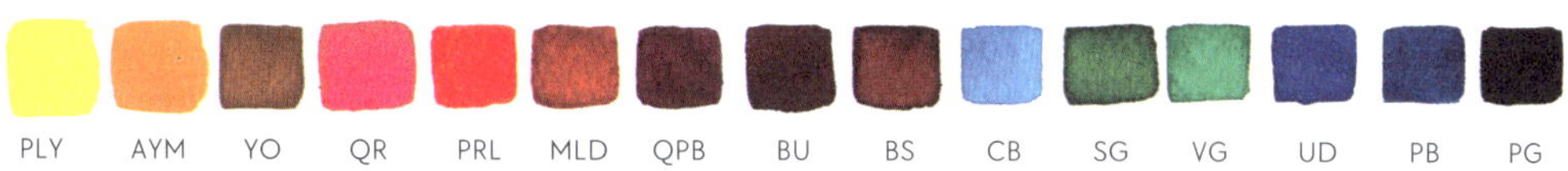

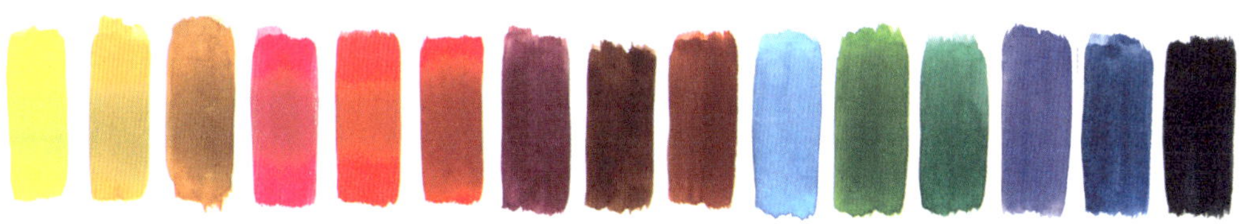

Although little watercolor pans are very practical and affordable, they can be quite concentrated, and the pigment can be tricky for beginners to use. If you struggle to get the paint out, lightly mist your pans with clean water.

When you're buying supplies, get yourself a small but high-quality palette and some additional tubes of other colors you particularly love or feel drawn to. If you end up painting regularly, you can invest in more tubes for basic colors and refill your pans with them instead of just buying more ready-made pans. Also, be careful when using dry watercolors, because they can drip onto the container and make the lid stick shut.

PALETTES

To use your paints, you will need a palette. I recommend a white palette with rounded hollows for the paint, since they are easier to clean than other types of palettes.

I personally like to use a white porcelain plate to mix my paints. I also use a plastic egg carton, because it lets me mix larger quantities of paint.

Choosing Quality

If you're just starting out, I recommend using few but high-quality materials. This will help you avoid issues that could quickly turn you off of painting with watercolors. Your choice of materials will depend on several factors: Will you paint often? Are you already a keen watercolorist? Do you want to paint in a sketchbook, on large-scale canvases, when you're out and about, or in the comfort of your own home? Think about which materials would transport well or be easier to work with inside or at home, and keep that in mind when making purchases. Throughout these pages, I let you know my personal favorite materials, but the best way to find what you like is by trying things out yourself.

Select Shades I Love

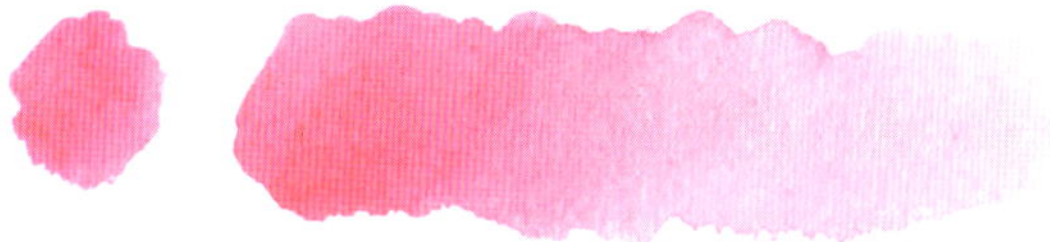

Opera pink
by Daniel Smith

Wisteria
by Daniel Smith

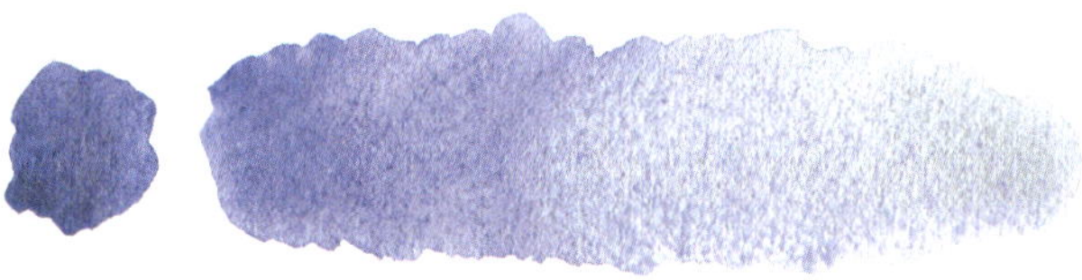

Lavender
by Daniel Smith

Aussie red-gold
by Daniel Smith

French vermilion
by Sennelier

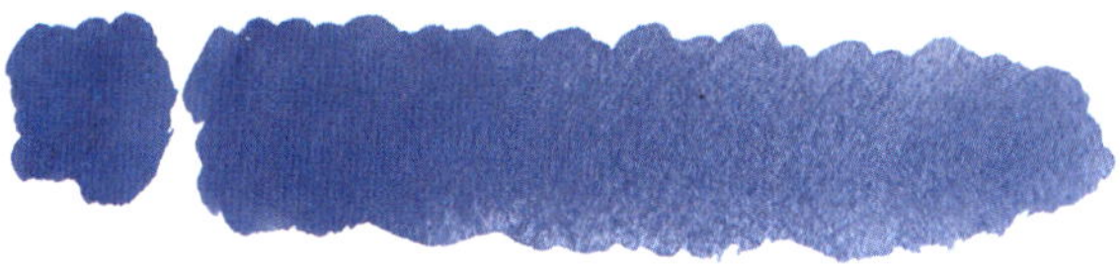

Cobalt blue hue (Bréhat)
by Dalbe

PAINTBRUSHES

PAINTBRUSHES CONSIST OF THREE PARTS: THE WOODEN HANDLE; THE HEAD, WHICH IS MADE UP OF HAIR OR BRISTLES; AND THE FERRULE, WHICH IS THE METAL BAND THAT HOLDS THE BRISTLES ONTO THE HANDLE. THE HEAD ITSELF IS SEPARATED INTO THREE SECTIONS: THE BELLY, WHICH IS THE MIDDLE; THE HEEL, WHICH IS THE LOWER PART WHERE THE BRISTLES MEET THE FERRULE; AND THE TIP, WHICH IS ALSO KNOWN AS THE TOE.

Here are four paintbrushes I recommend for your basic set:

- **Size #1 round brush:** Its narrow tip is perfect for finishes, details, and dry-on-dry techniques. 2
- **Size #4 round brush:** This is a good general-purpose brush and is also good for techniques that use more water. 3
- **Sizes #4, #5, and/or #6 round synthetic brushes:** Since synthetic bristles are stronger, they are more responsive to the touch than natural-hair bristles. Synthetic brushes can be used to lift paint off sections to make them lighter, for areas of flat color, and for details. 5 6
- **Medium cat's-tongue brush (pictured) or Filbert brush:** This is great for areas of flat color, to wet the paper, and for medium-thick brushstrokes. 7

You can also expand your collection with almost endless optional brushes. Here are a few specific ones I like to use:

- **A flat brush in a medium size (sizes #6–#9):** This will quickly fill areas and can give a crisp, straight line. 8
- **A size #1 Filbert brush.** Experiment with the kinds of marks it can make! 9
- **A size #10 Escoda Perla white synthetic round brush:** This is a particular favorite of mine because it is ideal for painting plants and landscapes due to its superfine tip. 10
- **A size #00 round brush:** A brush like this is great for the tiniest details. 1
- **A natural squirrel-hair brush:** Squirrel-hair bristles retain a lot of water, which makes them ideal for very fine details. They are also useful for mopping up excess water. 4

BRUSH CARE

Never leave your brushes sitting in water, because over time they will warp and the wood will start to crack.

Let your brushes dry with the head upright or lying flat, but make sure you rinse them properly first. Rinse them by rotating the head vigorously in water.

To take your brushes on the go, I recommend putting them in a small zip pouch and bundled with an elastic to protect the tips from damage.

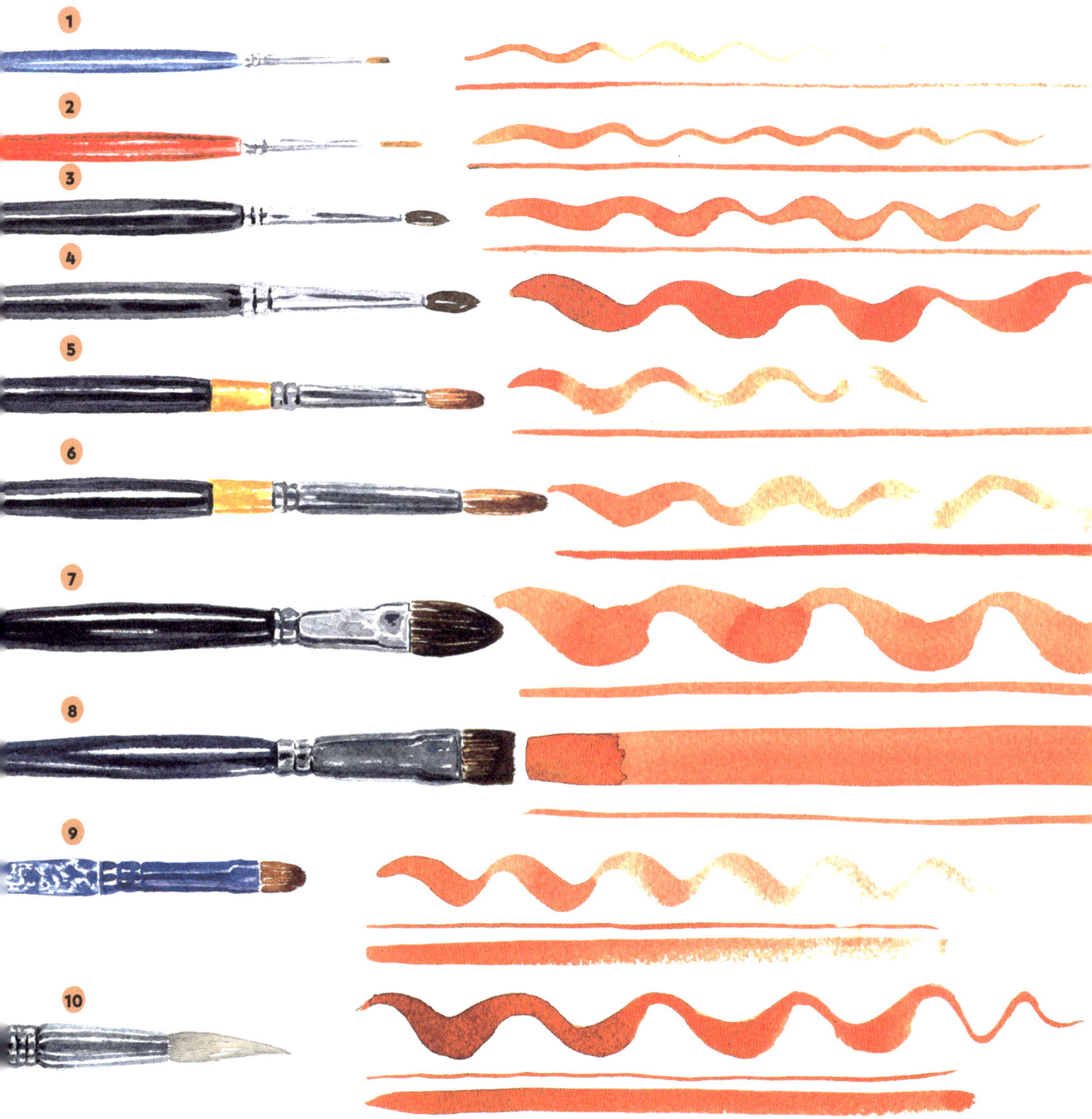
1
2
3
4
5
6
7
8
9
10

PAPER

Watercolor paper comes in different weights (thicknesses) and grains. I personally prefer to use fine-grain 300 gsm 100% cotton paper. Fine-grain paper allows for a beautiful and brightly colored rendering. I find that coarser grains give a slightly more muted look because the texture makes it difficult to accurately render details. Satin paper is too smooth, in my opinion, even though it allows for a great level of detail.

The best thing to do is to try out several types of paper to see which one you like best. Once you have used the same type of paper consistently over a period of time, you will learn how it behaves and can judge the outcome more accurately.

Even for practicing, I recommend steering clear of cellulose paper, because the result will be very different compared to what it would look like on cotton paper. Although cotton paper is more expensive, it has better absorption and thus dries more slowly, which gives you time to add beautiful light effects! On cellulose paper, which is denser, the water remains on the surface longer, which can cause pools, runs, and halos. Instead, use cellulose paper for color charts, quick sketches to warm up your wrist, or calligraphy.

Paper Formats

To achieve beautiful and delicious-looking pastry illustrations and take advantage of all the joys working with watercolors has to offer, I suggest going big. Most of my illustrations are at least 6 inches in size, though I often work with tabloid or A3-size sheets (about 11 x 17 inches).

For my drafts, I use an inexpensive A4 (approximately 8.5 x 11 inches) sketchbook that is made from certified FSC and responsibly sourced paper. It is just perfect for sketches and studies. Although it soaks up a lot of liquid and isn't meant to last a long time, any fluff can be easily rubbed off once the picture has dried, and it's not worth investing in thicker, more expensive paper just for practicing and sketching.

Another option that I love are the sketchbooks made by Etchr LAB, both in A4 (approximately 8.5 x 11 inches) and A5 (approximately 6 x 8 inches) formats. They are made from 100% cotton and are very beautiful, though they are a little more expensive than a standard sketchbook. The 250 gsm 100% cotton Watercolour Book by Hahnemühle is a similar option that's a little more affordable. Try to save money where you can in paper weight and quality as you build up your interest in the hobby, saving the best papers for your final works.

Your Painting Setup

When painting, you should raise your worktop by about 2 inches so that you can work more comfortably and so that the light won't cause as much reflection. You can do this by placing a wooden board, a block, or a box underneath your sketchbook, paper, or paper pad.

Since I'm right-handed, I have my paintbrushes at the ready to my right, resting on the lid of a tin, and my pencils on my left, so they don't roll under the board! If you're left-handed, you can set up your station in the opposite way, paintbrushes to the left and pencils to the right.

I recently invested in a sit-stand chair, and I'm very happy with it because it's easier on my lower back. This isn't something to gloss over. Once you sit down to paint, time passes quickly, and you can easily spend hours on end sitting, so it's important to make sure you're comfortable and supported!

ADDITIONAL MATERIALS

WATER

I use two containers of water: one to wet the paper, and another to rinse my brushes. Make sure to replace the water once it gets murky, because your colors will appear much duller if you don't keep the water clean.

Tip

Fill a small spray bottle with clean water and lightly spray your palette before use. You can also use this method to revive your dried paint mixtures on ceramic or plastic palettes.

CLOTHS

I always have a cloth handy to wipe off excess water from my brush or my painting. Make sure you wash such cloths regularly to avoid color transferring and stains. You can also use kitchen towels or microfiber cloths.

The Thumbnail Sketch

To get an idea of the structure and shape of a piece before painting it, make a small preparatory sketch in a square a little over 1 inch in size. This lets you visualize the light and shadows and create an intentional composition. Use a regular gray pencil and don't press down very hard with it, because it will leave marks on the paper.

Next, you can create a second thumbnail sketch in color on your chosen cotton paper so that you can choose and adjust your colors to be as pleasing and lovely together as can be! This will also help you overcome any fear of the blank page.

Try to keep an open mind and get out of your comfort zone, since it's all too easy to develop set drawing habits. Be open to the surprises the unknown may hold! This way, you will learn more and gain confidence in your artistic practice.

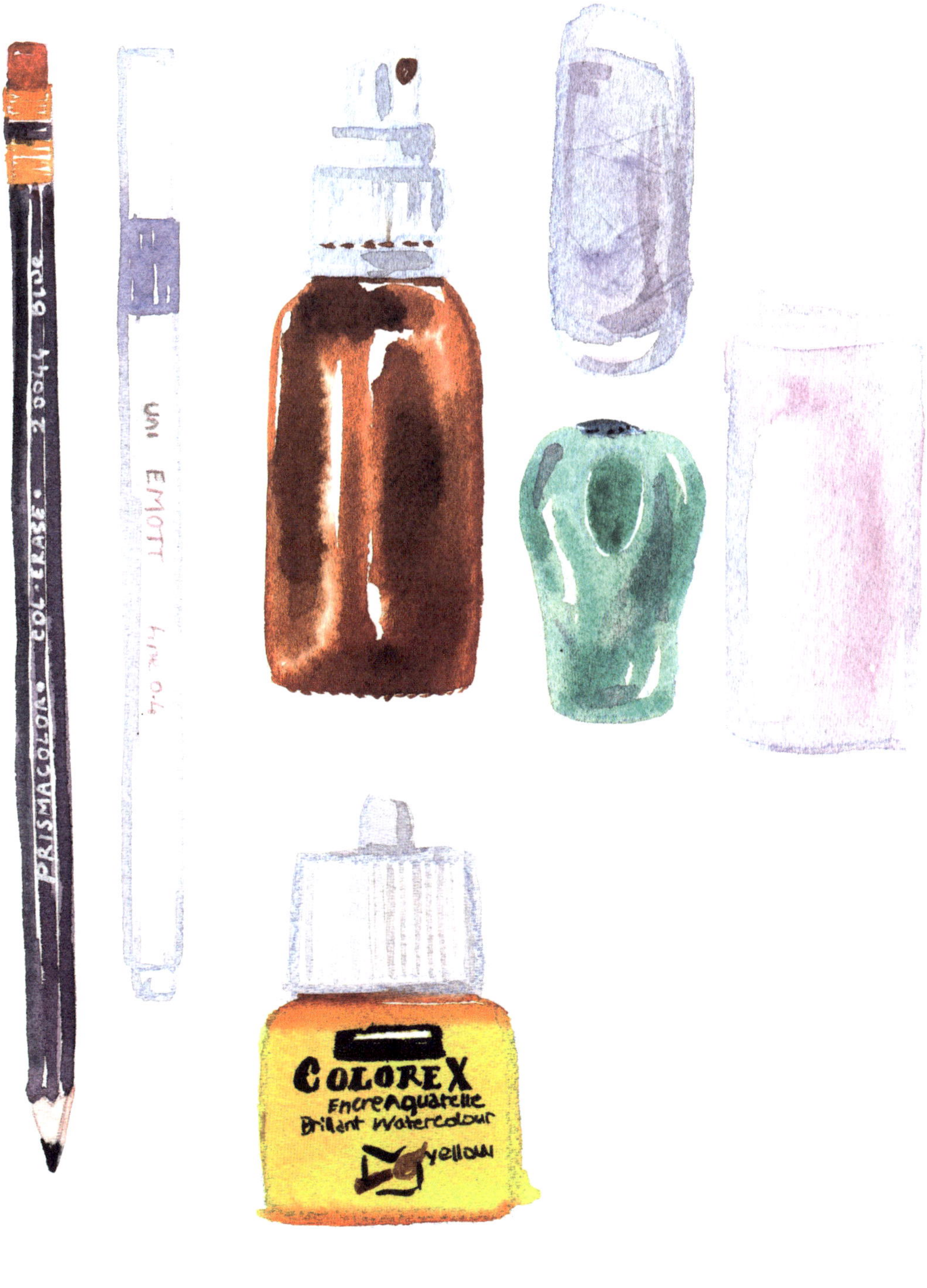
PRISMACOLOR• COL-ERASE• 20044 BLUE
uni EMOTT
COLOREX
Encre Aquarelle
Brillant Watercolour
yellow

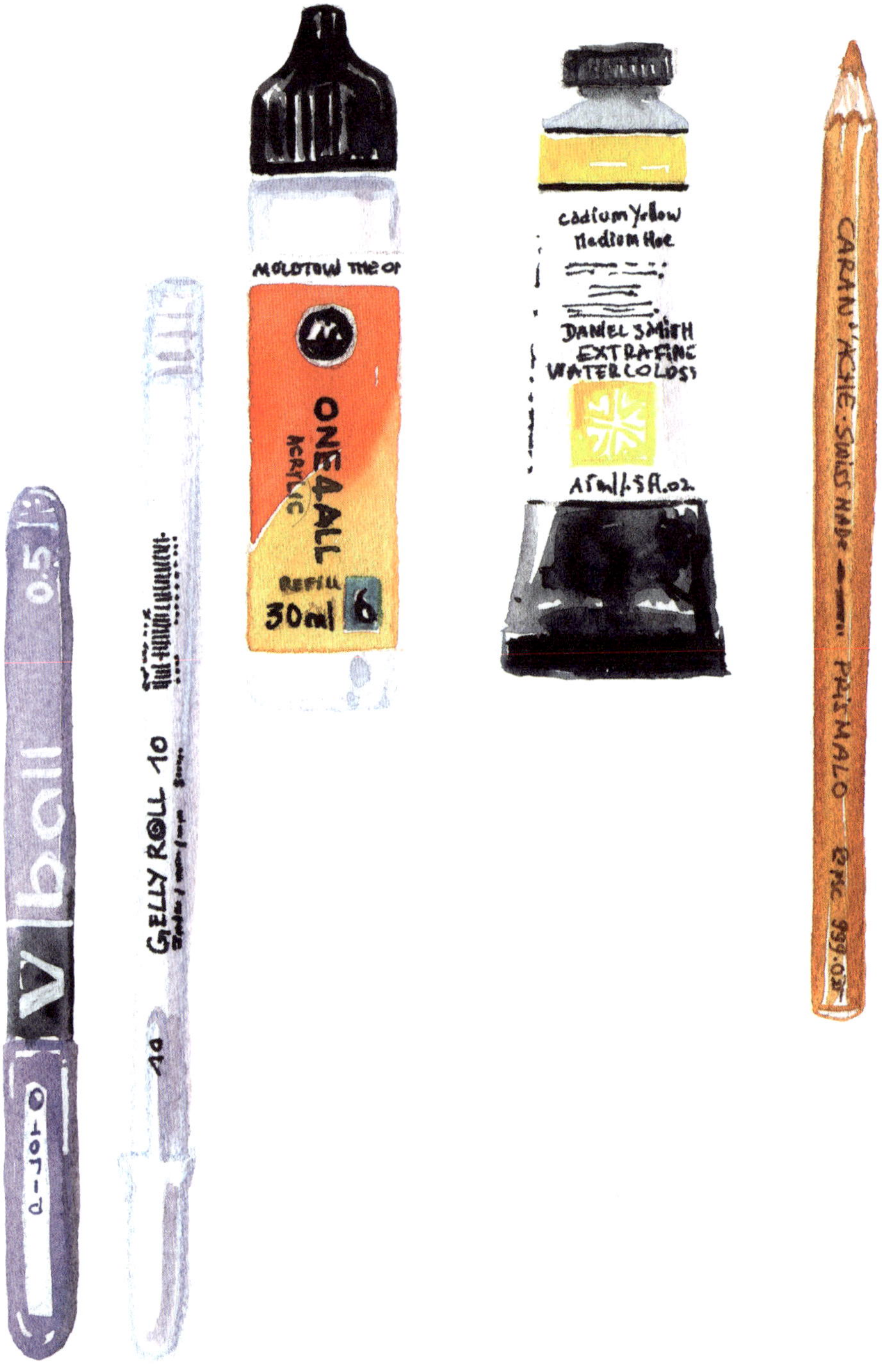
V ball
0.5
GELLY ROLL 10
ONE4ALL
ACRYLIC
REFILL
30ml
6
DANIEL SMITH
EXTRA FINE
PRISMALO

COLORED PENCILS

I like to make an under-drawing before I embark on painting my desserts, because it lets me visualize the depths of colors and balance my layout. My favorite pencil for this is the Prismacolor Col-Erase because it's erasable and does not blend with the paint like watercolor pencils do. It also doesn't leave dirty marks on the final painting, like conventional pencils do. Along with your colored pencils, make sure you have a kneaded eraser on hand.

INK

I like the intense effect watercolor inks can give. These are liquid watercolors in small vials that tend to be very highly pigmented. I find the Colorex drawing watercolor inks range by Pébéo very beautiful for the particular finishes I use them for. In this book, I used them for the donut sprinkles (page 90) and the candies (page 106).

OTHER TOOLS

Dig out a drawing compass from your school days to help with making round shapes for donuts or cookies. Use these as a basis to play around with irregular shapes with your watercolors.

You can use a toothpick (or a glass pen, if you have one!) to help create interesting textures on sweets, paint the wood of an ice-pop stick, paint patterns on leaves, or add grooves to certain doughs. Whether you're using a fancy glass pen or a simple toothpick, it works the same way: You use the tool to create a depression in the paper, and then the pigment settles in the groove, leaving a bold color line.

For white highlights, I use white gel pens. They are great for rendering powdered sugar and some of the details on cakes, for example. Two specific brands I like are the Gelly Roll 10 by Sakura and the Molotow One4all The Original refillable white acrylic marker.

Colored paint pens are also great for bringing out certain food decorations, such as sugar beads on donuts. I use Posca paint pens for this.

It's really up to you to find and mix techniques and tools to your heart's content, and to discover your personal style!

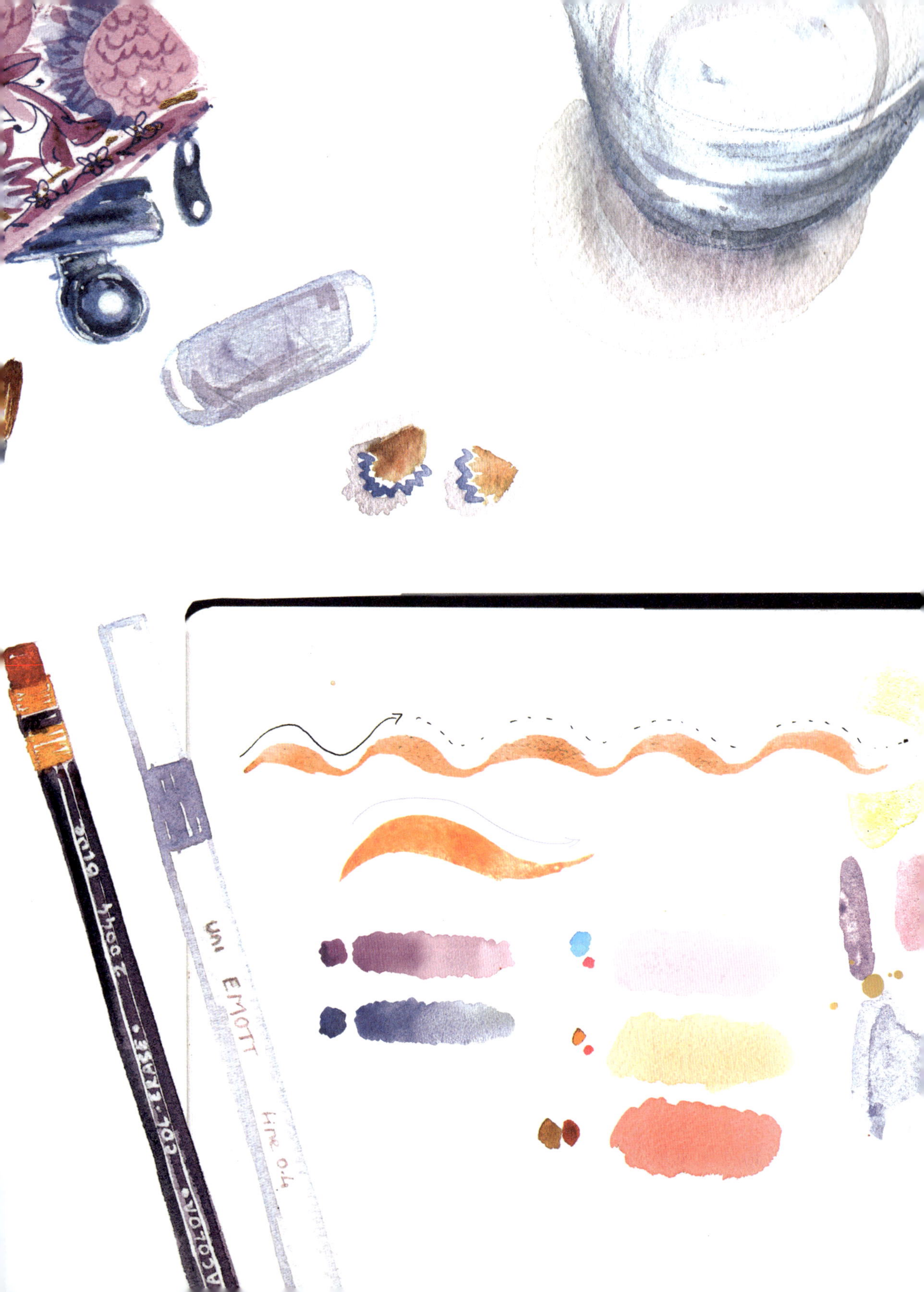
COL-ERASE
uni EMOTT
fine 0.4

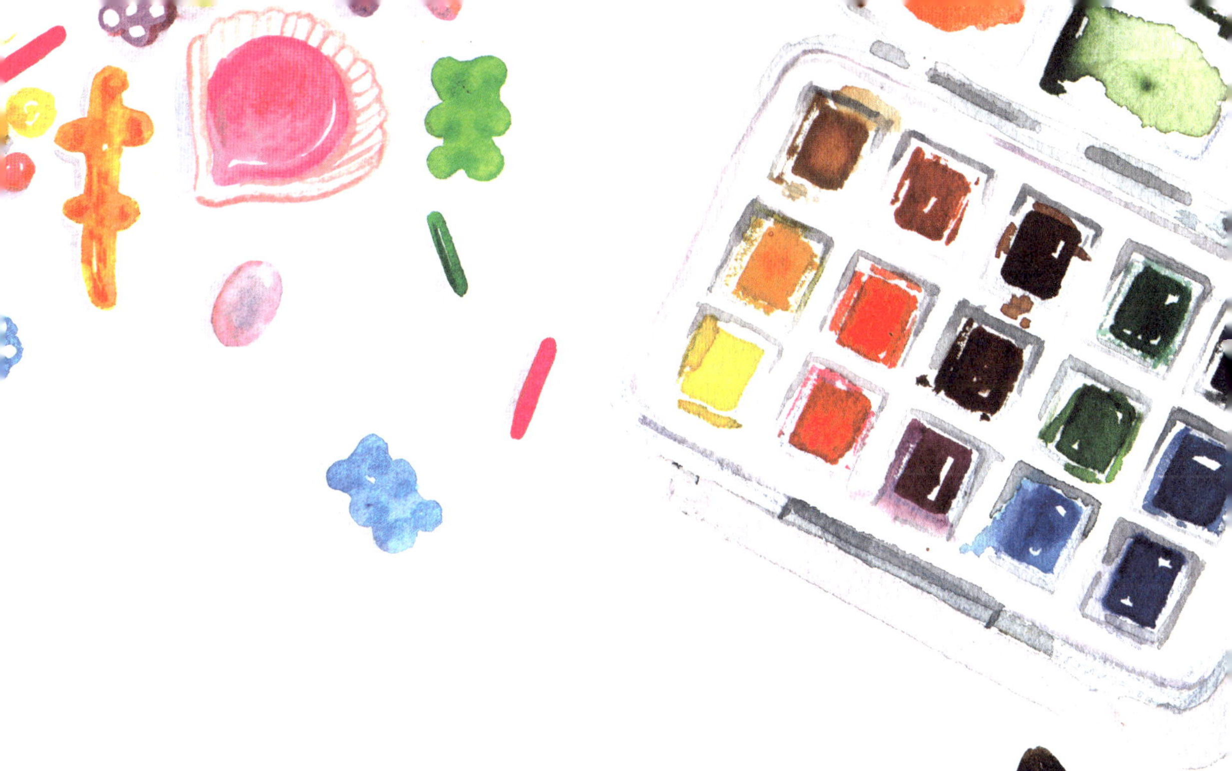

Basic Techniques

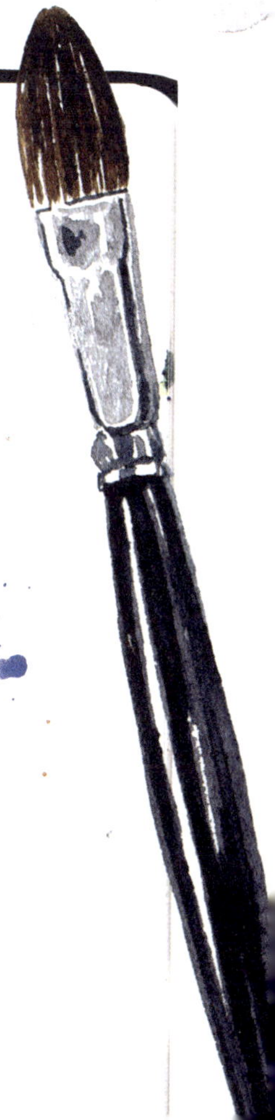

BRUSHSTROKES TO GET YOU STARTED

To get your paints ready, gently wet your pan with a wet brush or a spray bottle. Stir the paint in the pan in small, circular movements to let the pigment slowly dissolve, which will make it smooth and soft. If you paint with it at this point, the color will be intense and almost opaque. To start painting, wet your brush well, then remove excess water by lightly pressing it against the side of your water cup or a cloth or paper towel. When you are ready, you can dip it into the color in the pan.

Depending on what effect you would like to achieve, you can either paint with the tip of the brush by pressing down very lightly or do the opposite and use the whole brush head. Applying greater pressure will create a wider brushstroke. This can be useful for painting madeleines, leaves, or the light reflections on a donut, as well as when adding text to your creations.

Here are some practical exercises you can use to improve your brushstrokes.

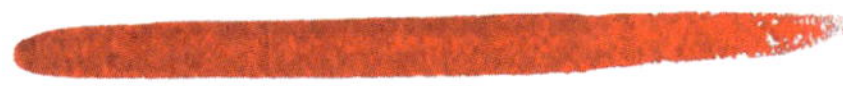

Pure brushstroke without rinsing first

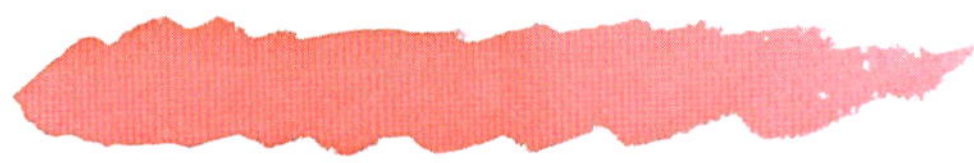

Wetted paint, light brushstroke

Wetted paint, firm brushstroke

Tip

Feel free to repeat these exercises whenever you are feeling uninspired or have 10 minutes to spare. The more you practice, the more progress you will make!

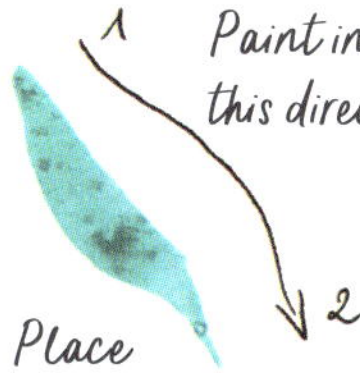

Place the brush, press, lift.

Paint in this direction.

Using the brush tip

→ Stroke direction

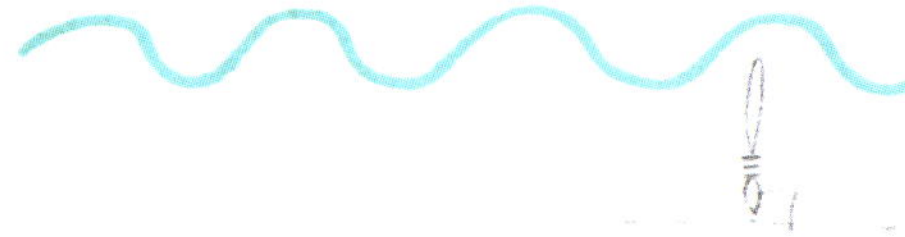

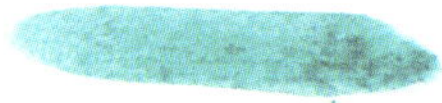

Using the brush belly

Press your brush head down fully.

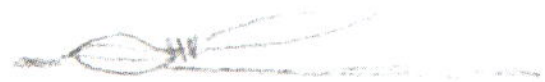

With the tip

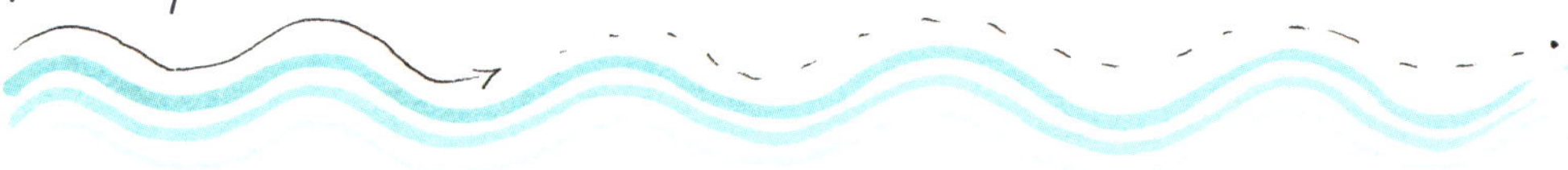

With the belly

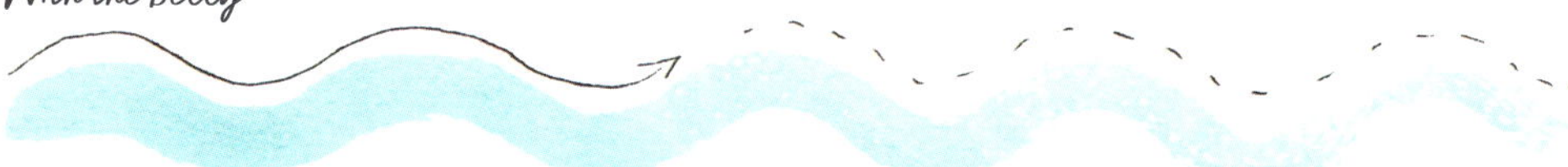

Alternating tip and belly

As the water gets absorbed, you can see more of the white of the paper.

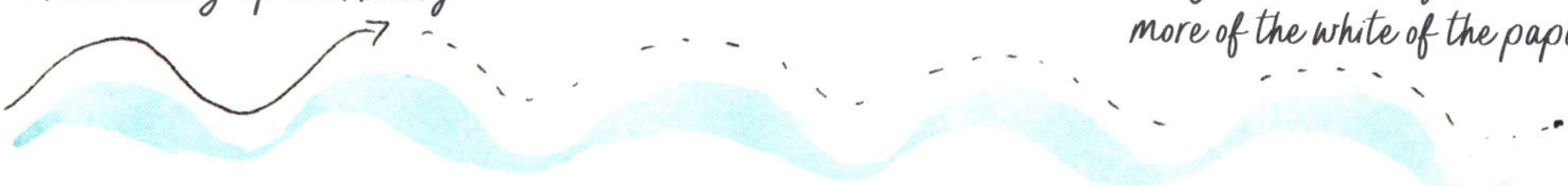

For the above three exercises, do not lift the brush off the paper as you make the stroke.

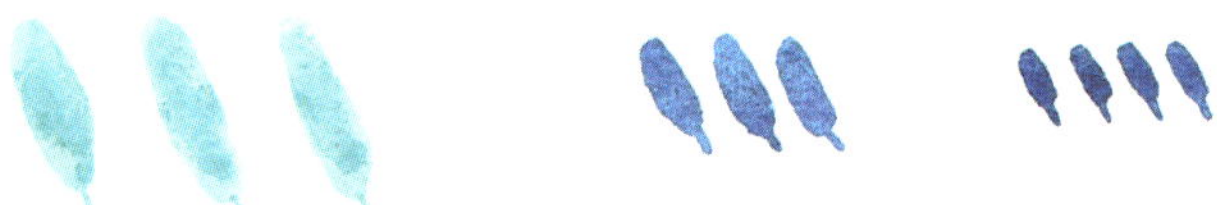

See what different natural shapes the brush makes when it's placed either fully or partially down on the paper.

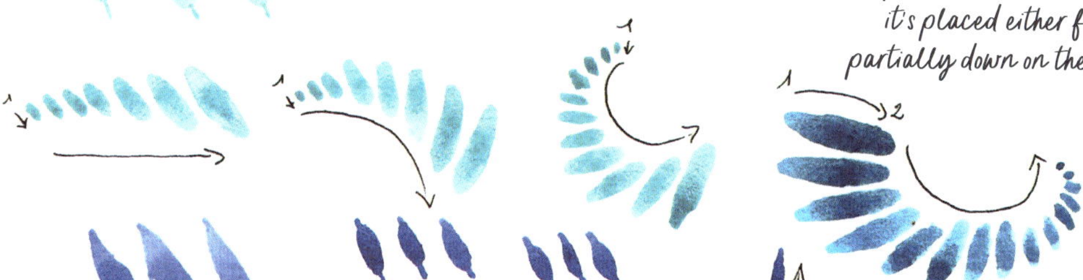

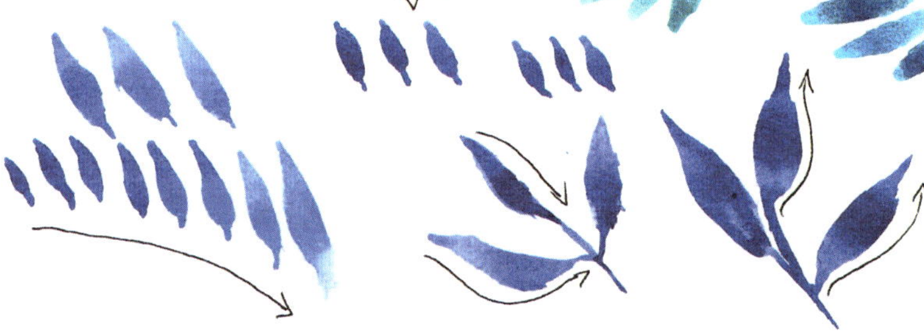

Change the direction of your brushstroke, move the paper around, and experiment!

WATERCOLORS AND WATER

UNDERSTANDING HOW BASIC WATERCOLOR TECHNIQUES USE WATER DIFFERENTLY IS IMPORTANT, SINCE WATERCOLORS—AS THE NAME SUGGESTS—CALL FOR WATER. THE BEST WAY TO ACHIEVE THIS IS PRACTICE, PRACTICE, PRACTICE. BELOW, WE'LL REVIEW THE ESSENTIAL TECHNIQUES SO YOU CAN SEE THE DIFFERENT RESULTS THEY EACH ACHIEVE.

DRY ON DRY

Paint a yellow spot. Wait until it has dried and then lay down a brush mark of pure red pigment (with very little water).

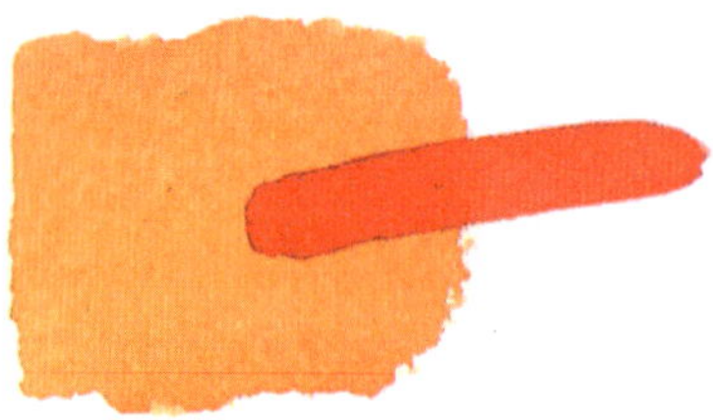

DRY ON WET

Paint a yellow spot. Before it has had a chance to dry, lay down a brush mark of pure red pigment (with very little water).

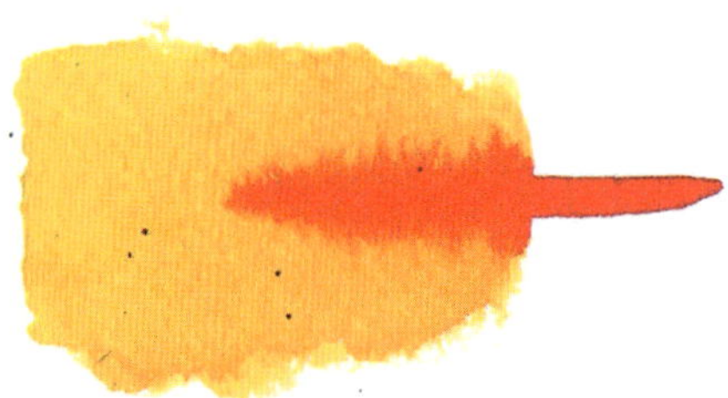

WET ON WET

Paint a yellow spot. Before it has had a chance to dry, lay down a brush mark of your prepared red paint (red pigment diluted with water). (Note: "wet on wet" refers to any time you put diluted paint down on top of a wet layer, whether the wet layer is a small or large area of wetted paper or a specific area of still-wet paint.)

WET ON DRY

The wet-on-dry technique is similar to what I consider to be glazing: adding a wet, diluted (and therefore not very pigmented) layer of color on top of an existing dry layer of color. Too much water can sometimes reactivate the dry paint below and create undesirable effects, though, so I typically do a very quick and light glaze if I'm using this method. Learn more on page 34.

You can do the same exercise shown here with any shape. You can also put paint down on simply wetted paper rather than on a layer of existing color.

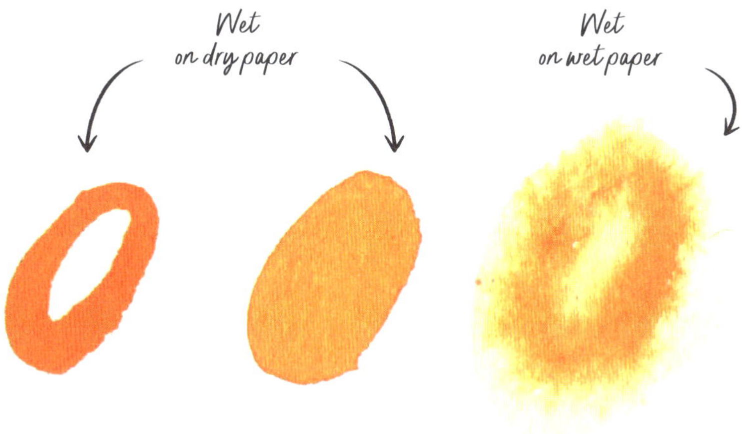

EXCESS WATER

Always mop up excess water on your sheet of paper; the water should never appear to be pooling when you look at your paper from an angle. All the water should have been absorbed, so you can still see the paper grain. If you place pigment on a surface that is oversaturated with water, the pigment will not reach all the way to the edge of the water and will become overly diluted.

THE COLOR WHEEL

PRIMARY AND SECONDARY COLORS

Red, yellow, and blue are called primary colors because they cannot be created by mixing other colors. Having said that, when painting with watercolors, it can be tricky to achieve certain nonprimary colors, such as opera pink or Aussie red gold.

When you mix any two primary colors in equal quantities, you get what's called the secondary colors: orange, green, and purple.

TERTIARY COLORS

There are six tertiary colors you can create by mixing a primary color with its neighboring secondary color:

- **Red orange:** vermilion or scarlet
- **Yellow orange:** ochre, gold, or saffron
- **Yellow green:** chartreuse or sulfur
- **Blue green:** turquoise
- **Blue purple:** indigo or bluebell blue
- **Red purple:** crimson

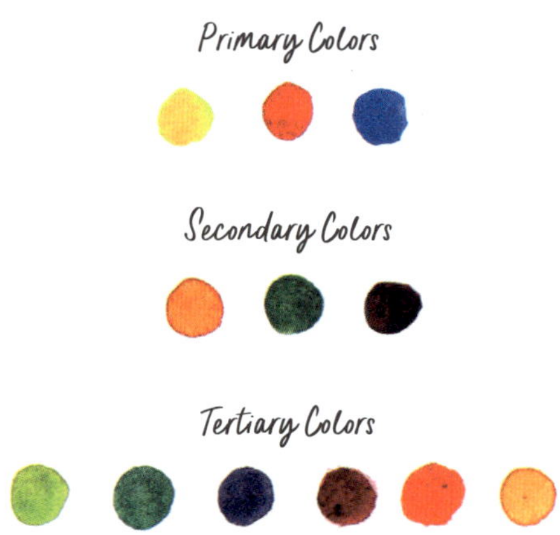

My Color Wheel

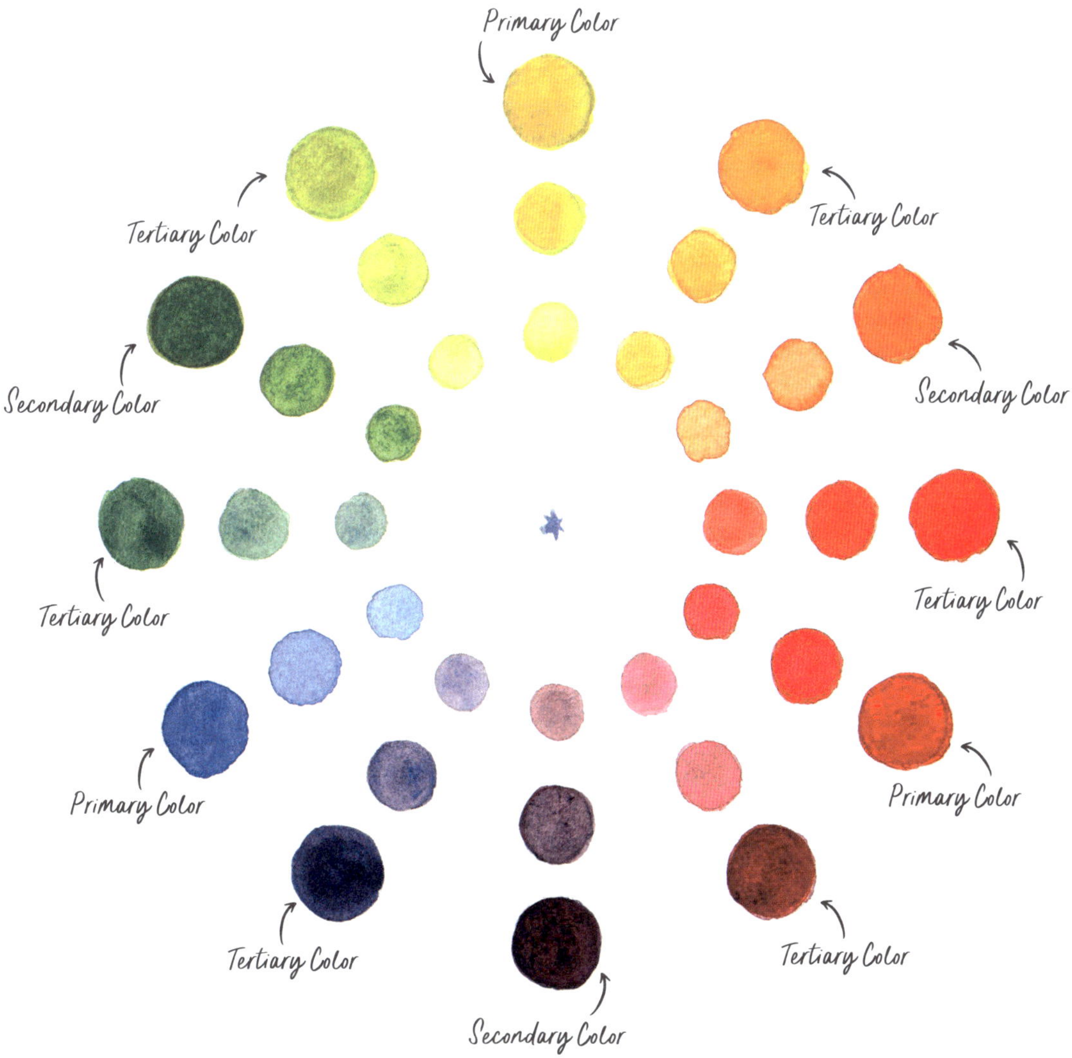

COLOR TERMINOLOGY

TEMPERATURE

There are warm colors and cool colors. Although we often split the color wheel into a warm side (red, yellow, pink) and a cool side (blue, green, purple), some reds are rather cool, and some blues are on the warmer side.

The more yellow you add to a color, the warmer it gets; the more blue you add, the cooler it becomes.

50 Shades of Pink

Consider the color pink: There are warm pinks—hues that are closer to orange (coral, powder pink, salmon pink), and there are cool pinks—hues that are closer to purple (fuchsia, raspberry, magenta, opera pink).

While you are out and about, in nature, in a store, or anywhere, take notice of colors in your surroundings and practice working out whether they are warm or cool.

When painting food, we use a lot of warm tones, which give a particularly appetizing look to the final result! In fact, different colors trigger different emotions in people. I prefer fresh, citrusy, and warm colors over muted and neutral shades, for example.

COMPLEMENTARY COLORS

On the color wheel, these are certain diametrically opposed colors. They exist in pairs, and each pair consists of a primary color and a secondary color (or two tertiary colors):

- Red and green
- Yellow and purple
- Blue and orange

In practice, using complementary colors adds a certain vivaciousness to your work. It can animate your piece or guide the onlooker's gaze to key areas.

In my illustrations, since I like yellow, I often deploy contrasts by using purple and blue. But there are many other examples! For Christmas illustrations, green and red give your work a certain twist: Red is highly visible against a green backdrop, since that is its complementary color.

You can also try pairings with cooler colors: a waffle on a blue plate, for example. To tone down the contrast of colors and create a fresher look, I opt for pink and green.

Just remember: There are no rules, so let yourself be guided by your imagination!

Exercise

Try painting variations of the same illustration by choosing different dominant colors, underlying shades, and so on, and then compare the effect this has. Have fun! Play and experiment!

MIXED PAINT

Distinct from the pure paint, mixed paint is simply the color you get when mixing watercolor pigments with water. The prepared mixed paint is often clear and transparent.

SATURATION

The more saturated a color is, the more vibrant and intense it is. A good example of this is my candy illustration on page 107. To make a color less saturated, mix into it a very small amount of its complementary shade or a neutral color.

COLOR MIXING

Mix your paints in a clean container and add small amounts of each pigment to start. Add more or less pigment of one hue or another and vary the water content to adjust the saturation of the color. The more water you add, the lighter the shade will be, and the more pigment you add, the more saturated it will be.

Most importantly, test your mixes on a small piece of scrap paper to see if you have created the shade you envisioned.

For ease, I prepare all my mixtures before I start painting. This is especially useful when you plan to be working using wet-on-wet or dry-on-wet techniques, or when you want to paint several of the same baked good.

Exercise

Practice making color charts for each color in your palette. Start the chart with the most saturated version of the color, then gradually add more water to your base mixture to get lighter shades. This way, you can vary the intensity of your colors and play around with transparency and depth.

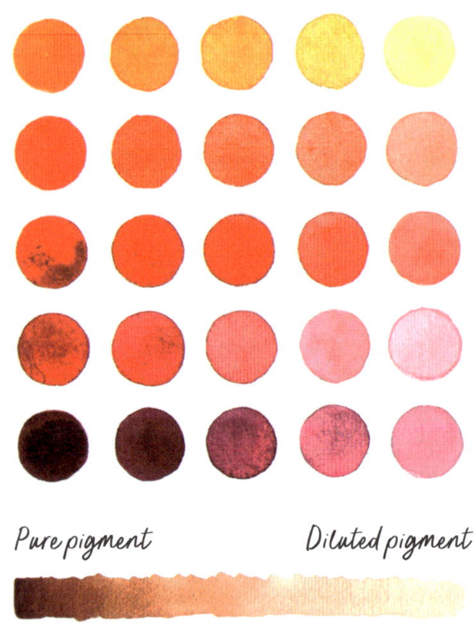

A good exercise for getting used to mixing and doing it more quickly is to understand colors and then reproduce them. For example, choose a color in an image and try to define its predominant hue; that is, the one that lends it the most pigment. Then ask yourself which colors you would need to add, and in what quantity, if you wanted to reproduce a lighter or darker shade: Would that color require more or less water (the core principle of diluting)? Would it need to be warmer or cooler? And so on. Refer to the color wheel if necessary.

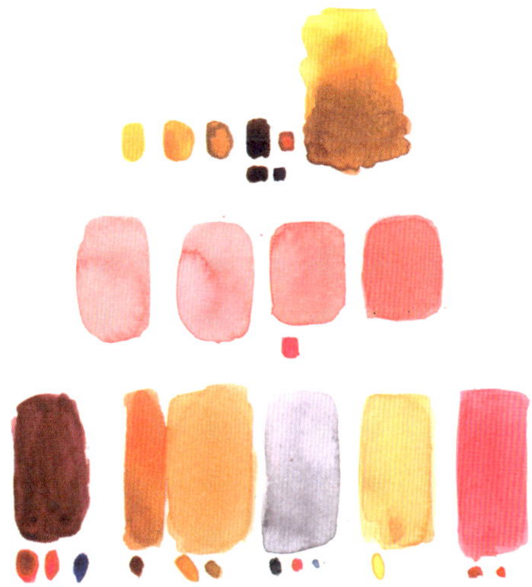

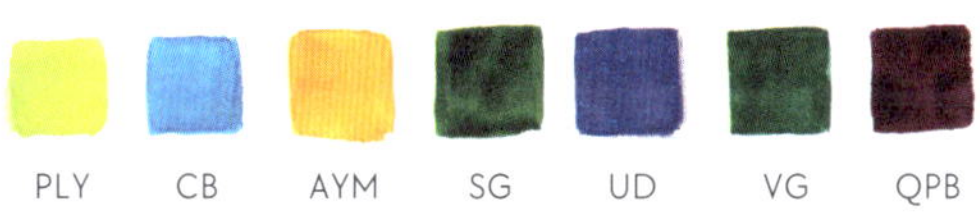

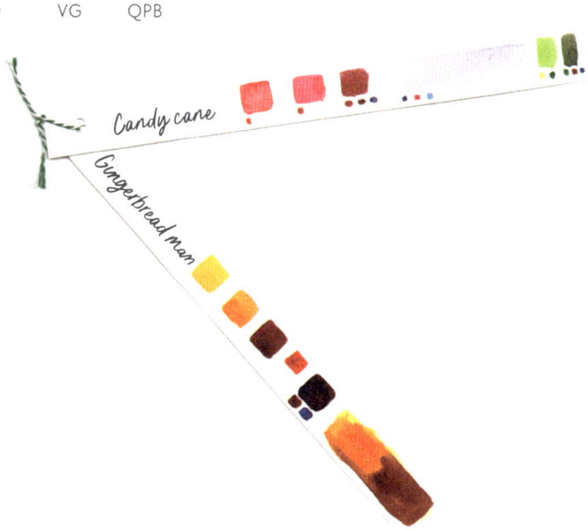

YUMMY COLORS

Here are some of the mixtures I use most often for painting pastries. Use the first color in each combination as your starting point and add the subsequent colors in varying quantities depending on the size of the surface you're painting. Always begin with small amounts of pigment and add more as needed.

You might want to have your sketchbook handy to do some studies and take notes. I sometimes refer back to these guides several times to get the right shade, even though I know my mixtures by now.

Feel free to interpret these in your own way, make them new, and find your own unique mixtures. At first, this may seem like a tedious task, but, with practice, it will flow more easily. Let's get started!

- *Milk chocolate* = yellow ochre + burnt sienna + burnt umber
- *Dark chocolate* = burnt umber + burnt sienna + ultramarine deep
- *Caramel* = yellow ochre + permanent red light + azo yellow medium + burnt sienna
- *Shortbread cookie* = burnt sienna + yellow ochre
- *Strawberry* = quinacridone rose + permanent red light
- *Raspberry* = quinacridone rose + permanent red light + madder lake deep
- *Blueberry* = quinacridone rose + ultramarine deep
- *Light shadow* = cerulean blue + quinacridone rose
- *Dark shadow* = ultramarine deep + quinacridone rose + burnt sienna
- *Sorbet* = permanent lemon yellow + sap green
- *Whipped cream* = cerulean blue + quinacridone rose
- *Cream* = yellow ochre + quinacridone rose
- *Pink powdered sugar* = yellow ochre + permanent red light (a larger quantity)

Mixtures with very little water

Mixtures with lots of water

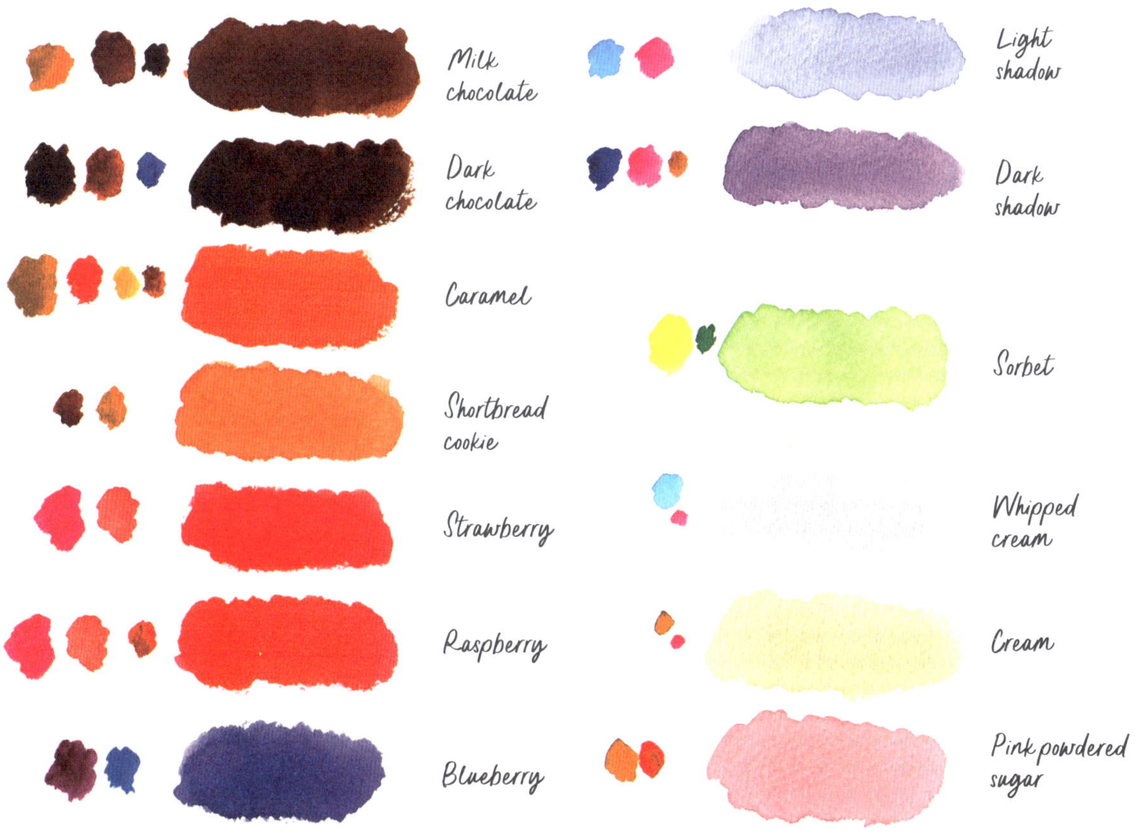

FLAT WASHES AND GLAZES

Flat washes or wash drawings (areas of flat, solid color) are layers of color applied evenly on a surface.

Flat washes can form the backdrop of a painting or simply fill a fairly large area within a panting. You can also create a pretty gradient by using several colors blended into one another. I rarely use this technique for painting pastries, although I find it useful for painting landscapes.

The colors of these wash drawings can be warm, cool, or even variegated if you're using more than one color. Once you have wetted your paper, you must work quickly to add color using long brushstrokes.

Glazing is another technique I often use; it is applying one layer of color on top of another.

Since watercolor is transparent, the first layer of color remains visible even when applying a glaze on top. I use this technique to create eye-catching reflections. Once the composition has dried, a glaze can brighten up areas of light, making a muted color warmer or reinforcing an area that is too light.

Cool flat wash

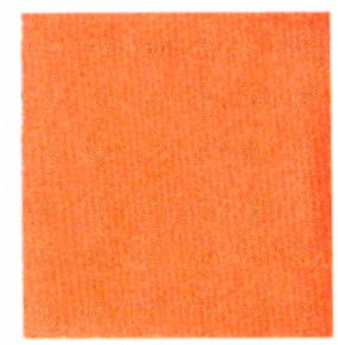

Warm flat wash

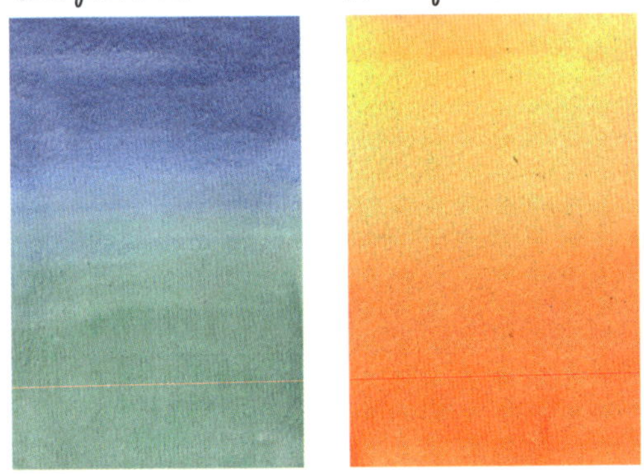

Variegated wash using two colors

Tip

Watercolor loses about 30% of its color saturation during the drying process. That's why this technique is so useful for realistically depicting sweet treats, since many of them have delicate, slightly muted colors.

BLANK SPACE

Blank space is very important in watercolor painting, since the white of the paper will help bring your sweet treats to life.

From the very beginning, you should think about the direction of the light: Which side does the light shine from in your drawing? This will determine where you will leave a blank space, even if you decide to partially fill it later on when your painting is almost finished. When you have worked out the angle of the light, you can place your shadows accordingly.

But don't panic if you're worried about accidentally painting where you shouldn't: You can always resort to your masking fluid—see the next page!

Tip

Sometimes, for ease and speed, I leave a narrow, blank gap when painting using wet-on-wet or dry-on-wet techniques. This prevents transparent colors from overlapping or running into one another. Once the watercolors are perfectly dry, I sometimes fill in the gap with another layer of paint.

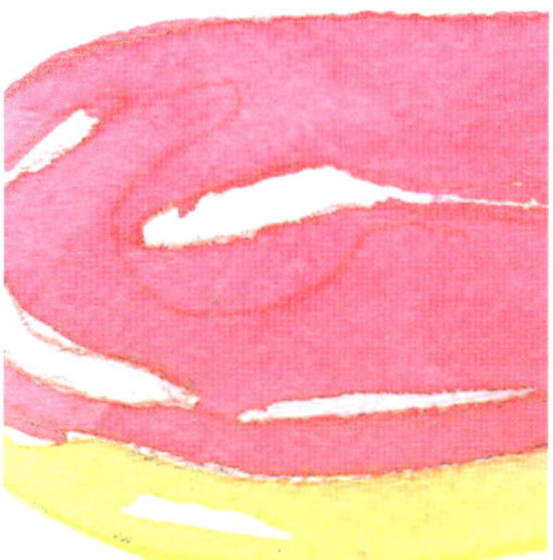

MASKING FLUID

Masking fluid, also known as drawing gum, keeps areas white by preventing the watercolor paint from getting into the paper.

Even though I prefer the technique of leaving areas on the paper unpainted, I still use masking fluid in specific situations: to make powdered sugar, a zigzag of cream, or dripping frosting. You can use masking fluid that comes in a pot or in a pen.

To apply masking fluid from a pot, grab an old synthetic brush you don't use anymore and dip it in soap. This will protect the bristles. Do not use this brush to paint again afterwards—only use it for masking fluid.

Make sure to factor in a longer or shorter drying time depending on the size of the masked surface. Note, though, that the masking fluid must not be left on the paper for too long, because it will turn sticky.

Once your painting is finished and dry, you can remove the masking fluid by gently rubbing it off with your finger or with an eraser.

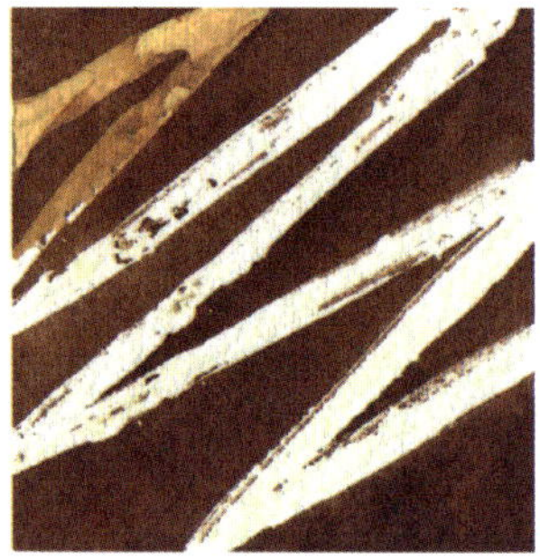

Tip

Masking fluid can also be used on top of color, as shown in this example.

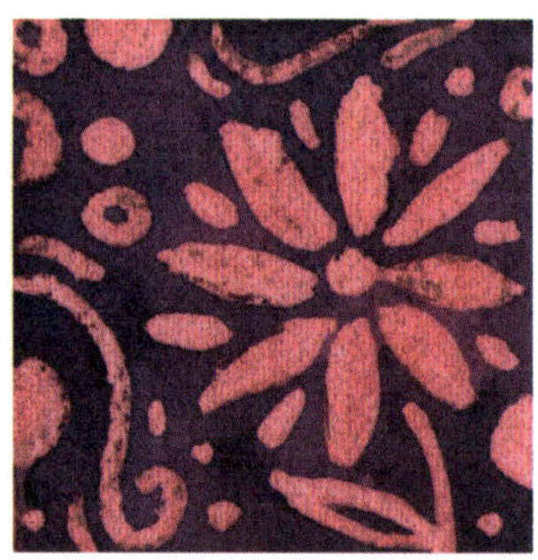

LIFTING

Similar to when leaving blank spaces, you can create highlights by removing some of the paint you have already applied. This technique is called lifting, and it requires a steady hand and patience.

Stroke over the wet area from which you want to remove the color by using a dry brush. Use a Filbert brush with a tapered tip for small areas or those that need to come out very white, and use a softer brush if you want a gentler, more blended effect.

Dry your brush after each stroke and repeat the movement until the area is lighter. I sometimes repeat this several times to make sure the section is as light as I would like it to be. Alternatively, to remove color from an already-dry section, use a damp brush.

You can use the lifting technique to blur the edges of a shape if you find them to be too harsh, or to soften a blank space created with masking fluid.

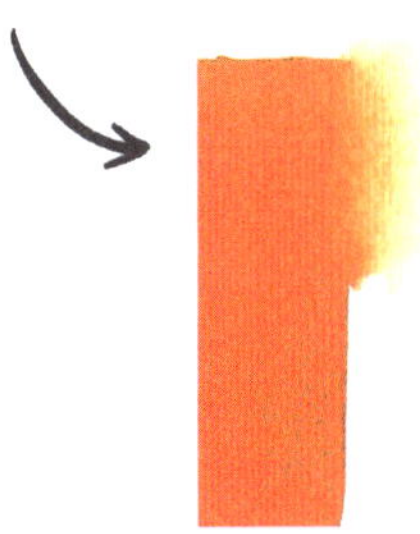

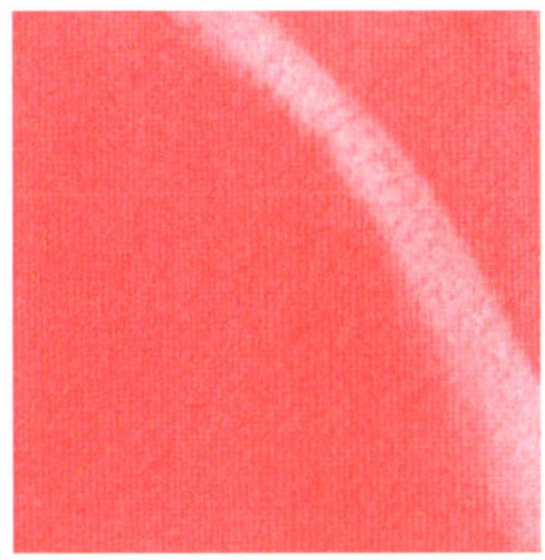

Remember that if a drop of water falls onto a colored surface, the water will disperse the pigments and create water blooms.

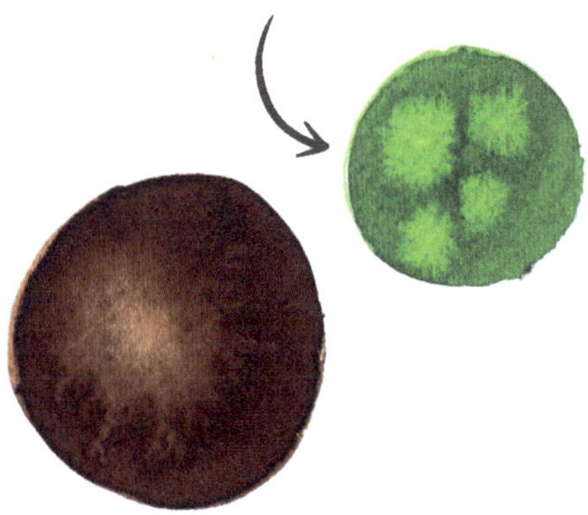

BLENDING

Blending is when you merge two or more pigments by using water. This gives a blurred, misty, and elusive appearance to the shape. On wet paper, the shape will become blurred. On dry paper, it will be crisp and precise.

If the area is still moist, you can also add some pigments of another color or of the same color to increase its intensity. These will mix with the color on the paper if the paper has not yet dried. This livens up your creation and lets you play around with textures (for example, for melting ice cream, soft or crunchy textures, and so on).

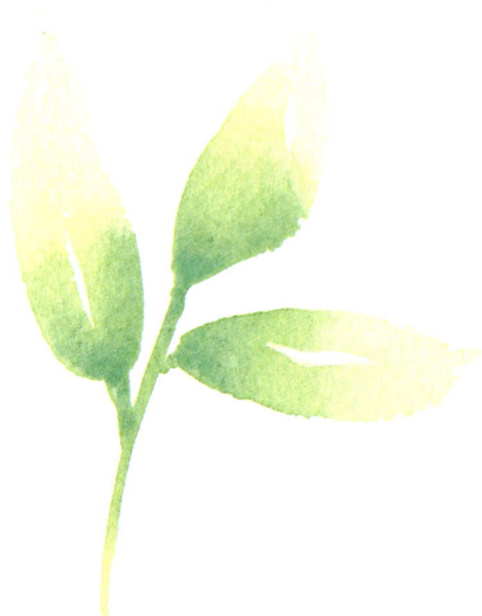

Exercise

Draw leaves with a brush dipped in clean water. Add a touch of green to the stem and the tip of the leaves. Through blending, the color will spread and flow, following the water to stain the leaf.

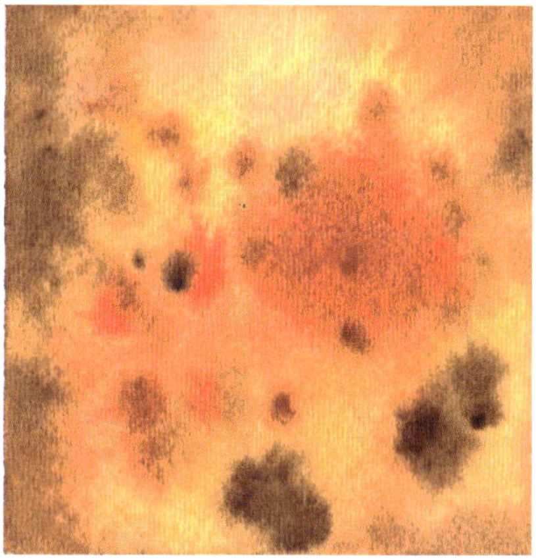

Exercise

Try the previous exercise with a line of water instead of leaves. Observe how the pigments spread along this line.

Now drop some water onto your sheet using a brush, but don't let it bead! Then drop a few droplets of pigment here and there. Watch what happens!

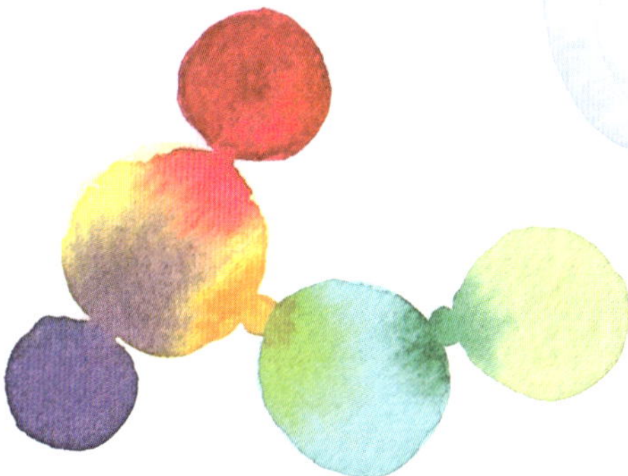

SPLATTERS

Splatters create a beautiful effect and add a unique energy. I always keep several sheets of scrap paper next to my workstation to cover sections and protect them from splatters.

I use different brushes when splattering that I dip either in pure or diluted color.

- **Using a small brush:** To create spots in a defined area, tap the ferrule near the head of the brush. This technique is perfect for depicting powdered sugar or the texture inside a cake.

On a dry surface

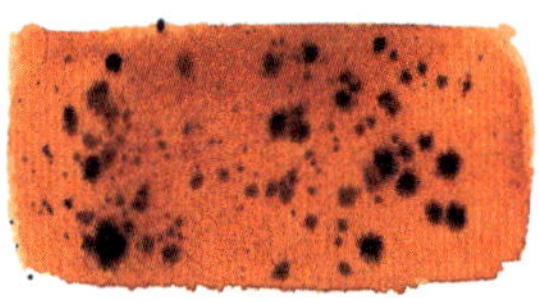

On a wet surface

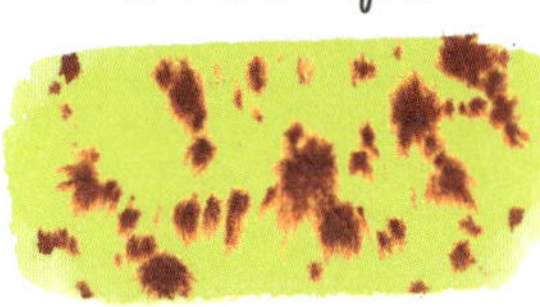

On a wet, lighter surface

- **Using a toothbrush:** This creates much-finer droplets that spread far and wide, so use plenty of scrap paper sheets to protect the other areas of your painting!

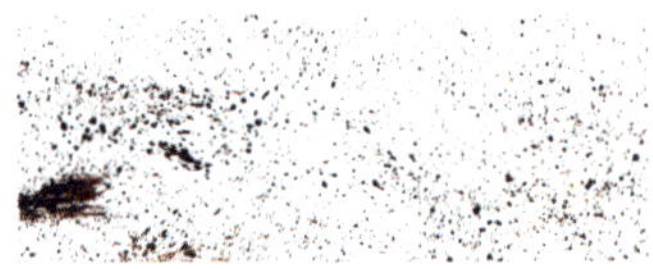

On a dry surface

- **Using a large watercolor brush loaded with plenty of water and pigment:** This leaves larger spots, especially if you tap the brush handle. This method is ideal for painting ice pops or adding a dynamic sense to your illustration.

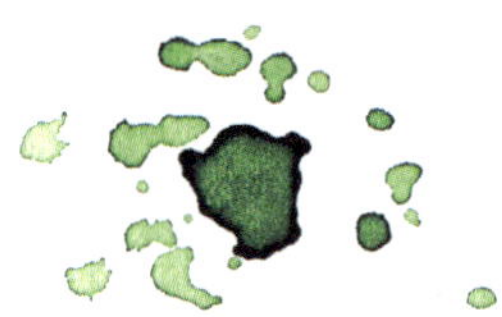

Spots with diluted mixed paint

- Instead of watercolor paint, you can also use white acrylic paint on wet or dry paper to achieve a similar effect.

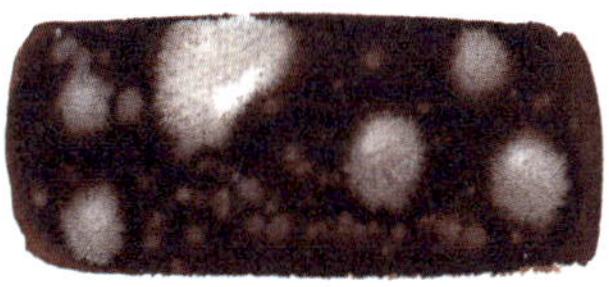

Acrylic on wet

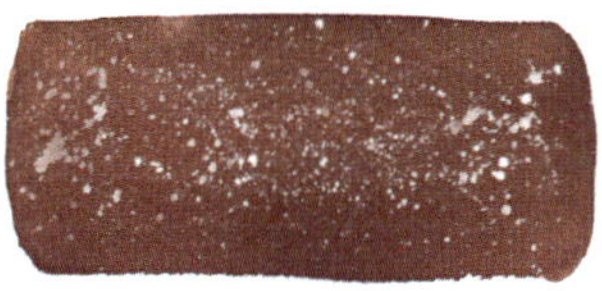

Acrylic on dry

- You can also create splatters with just water!

Clean water spots

Fixing Errors

If you accidentally leave a stain, don't panic. You can blot it and then use the lifting technique to mop up the paint with clean water.

If you think you have indeed made an irreversible mistake, try to look at your painting with fresh eyes to come to terms with or even appreciate it. You can also try to redo the same design differently. I suggest keeping all of your paintings and dating them to remind yourself of the progress you've made.

CREATIVITY AND INSPIRATION

The questions we ask ourselves as we start creating take us on a journey in their own right. Developing your own style will come from practice just as much as it will come from what inspires you. The things that fulfill you in your everyday life, the gifts and surprises life has in store for you, and your ability to be moved are what nourish your artistic style and give you inspiration.

To train your mind in the art of creativity, it's important to avoid a few pitfalls that can stand in the way of you reaching your full potential:

- Being too much of a perfectionist and wanting to control everything
- Drawing with a bad setup or in uncomfortable conditions, painting too fast, choosing a subject that is too complicated, or expecting a very precise result, which is, in a way, the opposite of what watercolor painting will provide
- Being afraid to fail and comparing yourself to others
- Becoming obsessed with social media—the aim is not to produce for the sake of producing or to receive attention, and comments from people online should almost never be taken seriously!

Instead, it is key to establish an environment that stimulates your creativity.

- Observe, contemplate, marvel at beauty and harmony, and take the time to notice the small things in life. In short, nurture the things that bring you joy!
- Let go, be at peace with yourself, and let yourself be guided by your inner voice to live fully in the present moment. For example, you could practice meditation and relaxation techniques, since creativity is as much driven by the voice inside you as it is by external elements. Practicing watercolor painting will help with this.
- Stay organized and tidy, since a clutter-free workspace invites the freedom and spontaneity you need to find inspiration.
- Get bored! Switch off your phone and don't let yourself get distracted by this world that never stops. Your mind often comes up with the best ideas when you remove all the unnecessary outside stimuli.
- Dedicate time to what brings you joy, whether that is visiting museums, traveling, gardening, cooking, reading, listening to music, meeting friends, listening to podcasts, going to the cinema, taking a walk, or even booking an eating-and-walking tour. Intentionally taking actions like these can get the creative juices flowing!

- Listen to yourself—think about what you enjoy, your artistic style, your interests, your likes, and your dislikes.
- Carry around a notebook when you're out and about to take notes on the things you notice in your surroundings. This will help you recall images, scents, sounds, and feelings that you can use to form ideas. You can do this in a sketchbook, on your phone, or even in a voice memo. Don't be afraid to doodle or sketch alongside your notes as well!
- Share your passion and your art by joining a community on social media, exchanging ideas with like-minded people, or engaging meaningfully with others in any way you can think of to. A good way to get into contact with other people is by painting outdoors. It's an artistic adventure, since you have to choose your materials and pack them for use on the go, but it also offers the possibility of human connection, which makes the chaotic nature of everyday life recede into the background.
- Let yourself be inspired by creating mood boards on Pinterest or in any other creative app you like. You can also create mood boards by collaging in a sketchbook! You can start by finding an image that speaks to you and "copying" it to learn a technique, capture a certain light, master an effect, and so on (but remember to credit the original artist if you decide to make your painting public in any way). This trick helps you learn to mix and combine several elements (composition, color palette, setting) to come up with your own, new work.

Above all, have fun and experiment! Practice gratitude and be gentle with yourself. There are no errors or defeats—only small steps on your path to developing further as an artist and as a person. Creation and love are closely linked—both are encounters with yourself and your inner child.

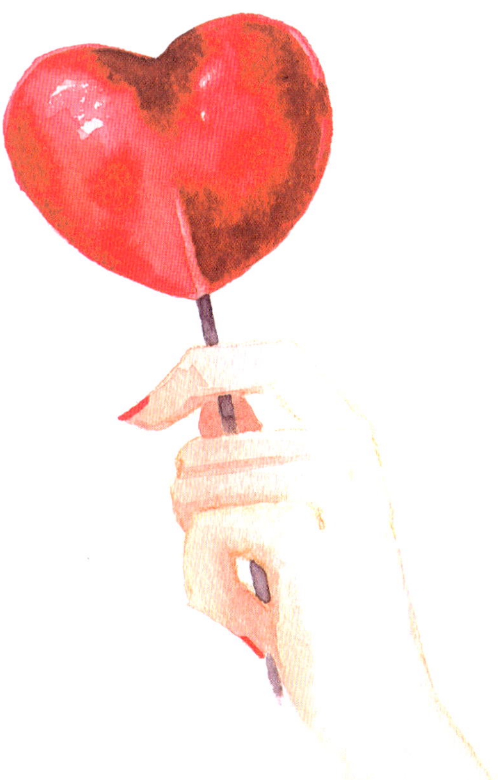

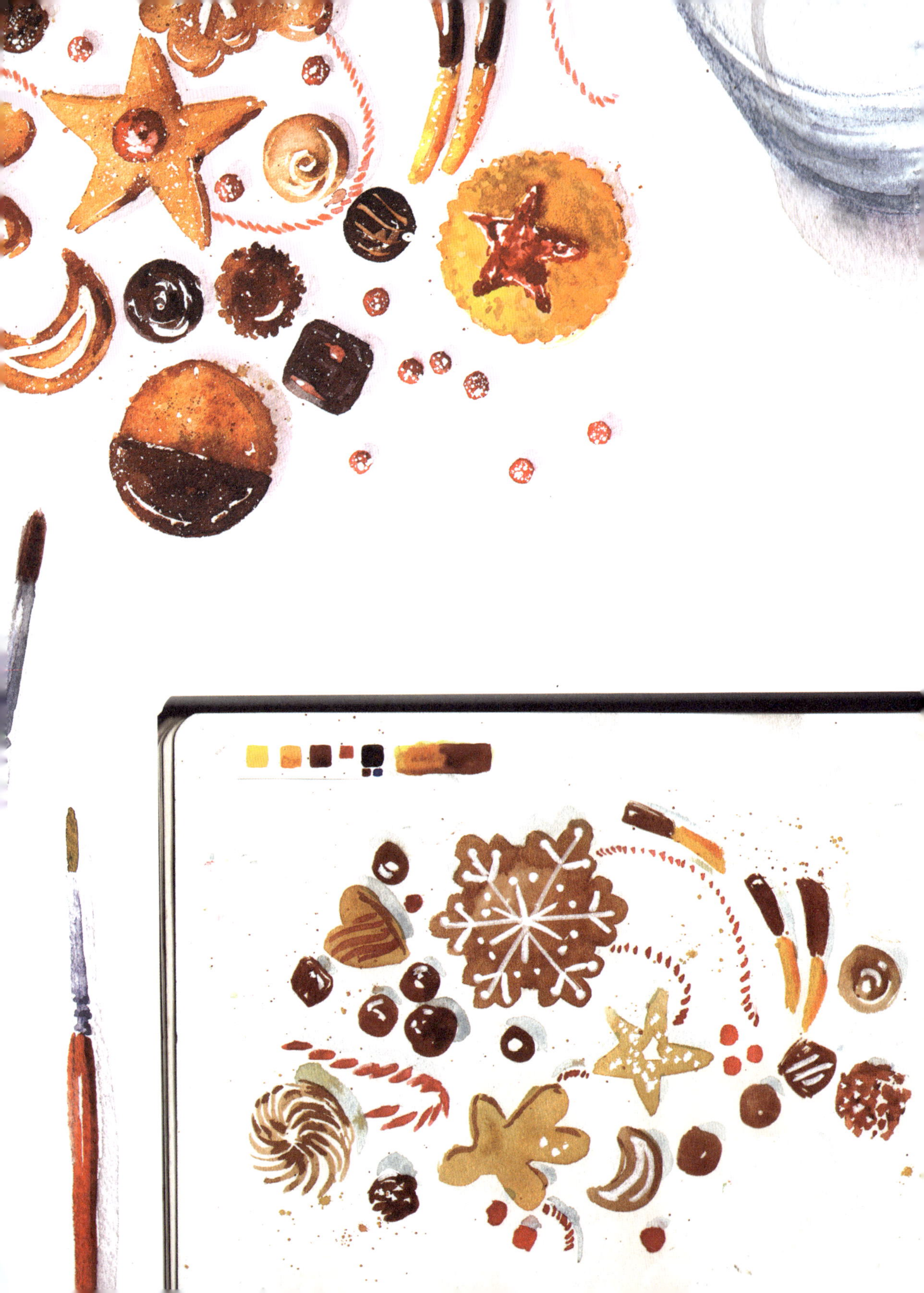

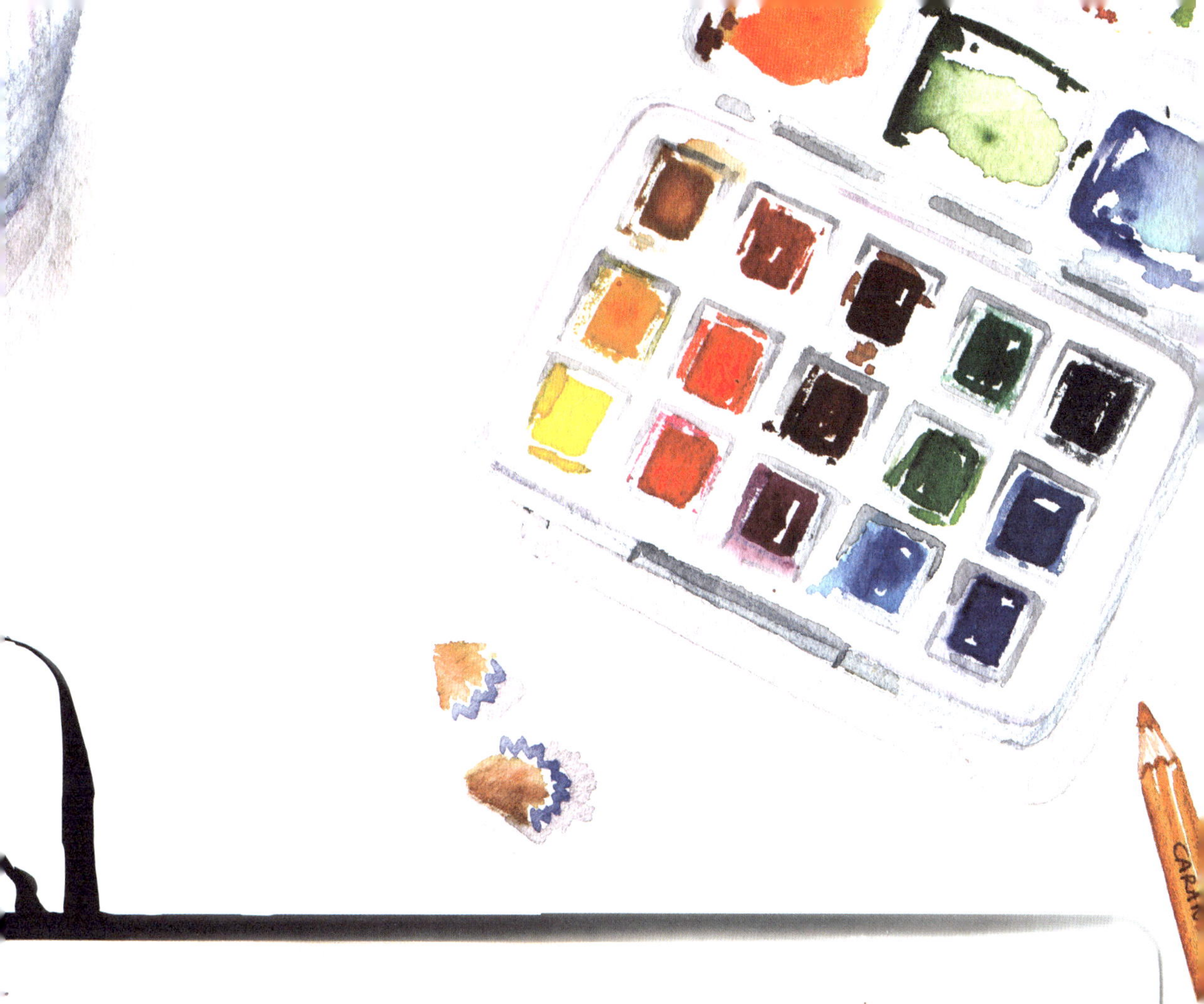

Delicious Delights to Paint

FLAVORS OF FALL

Inspiration

LEAVES ARE STARTING TO PILE UP ON THE SIDEWALK AND CRUNCH UNDER MY FEET WITH EVERY STEP. NATURE'S TRANSFORMATIONS PROVIDE SO MUCH INSPIRATION FOR PAINTING.

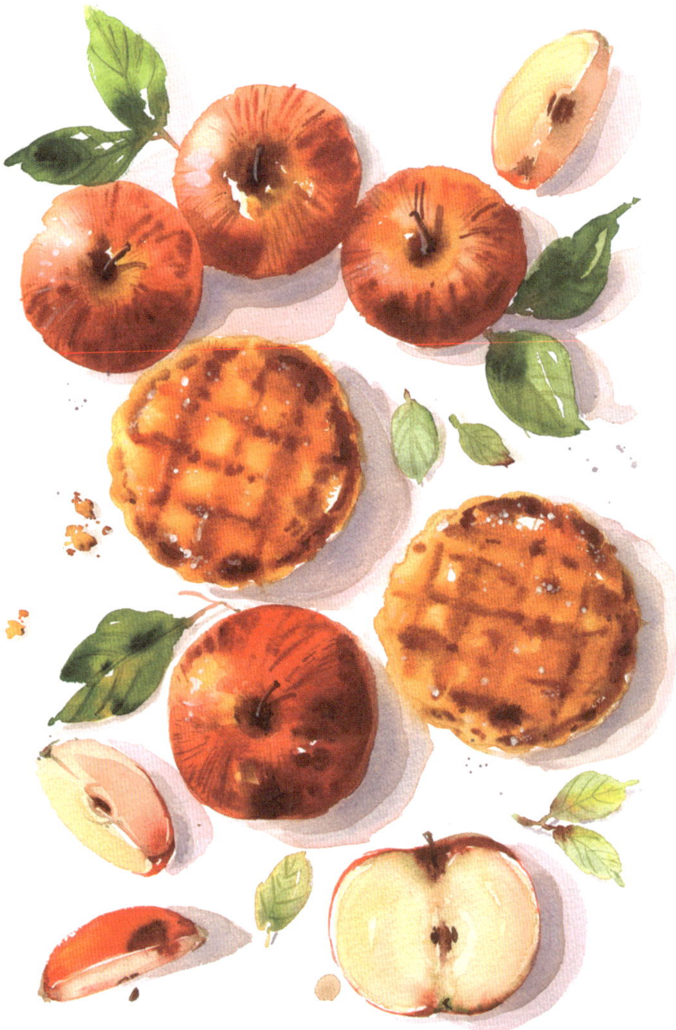

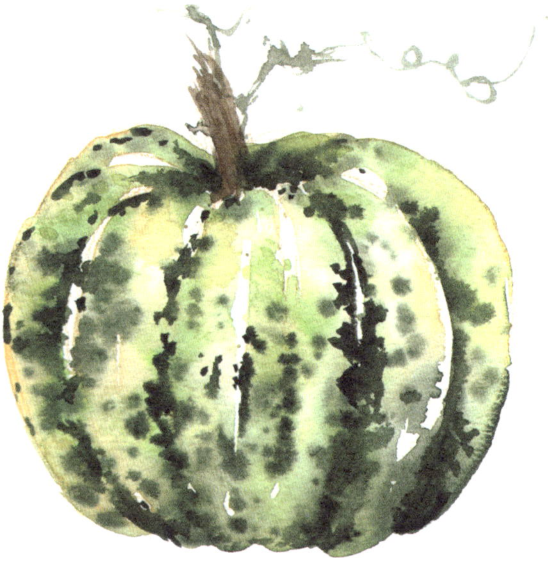

Ochre + cadmium yellow

Moss green + yellow

Sap green

Perylene green

Make sure you depict the grooves of a pumpkin by leaving some blank spaces between the segments.

Pumpkin orange

Orange + vermilion red

Orange + VR umber

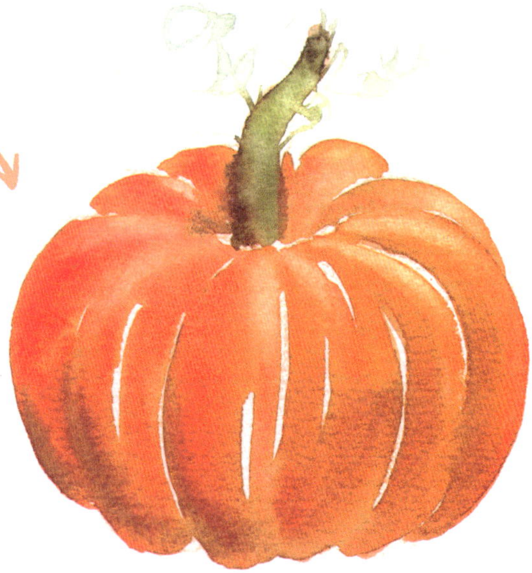

PUMPKIN SPICE LATTE

Step by Step

I LOVE LATTES, AND THIS ONE CELEBRATES THE FALL SEASON LIKE NOTHING ELSE. IT FEATURES A PUMPKIN-FLAVORED WHIPPED CREAM INFUSED WITH WARM SPICES LIKE CINNAMON, VANILLA, GINGER, AND NUTMEG—WHAT'S NOT TO LIKE?

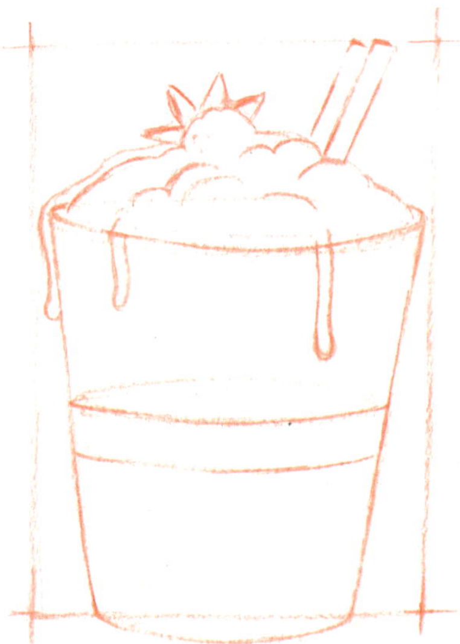

1 Start by sketching the glass for the pumpkin spice latte within a rectangular grid.

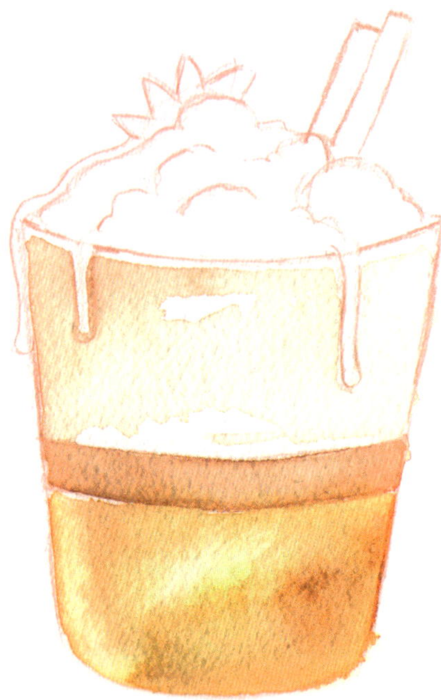

2 Working wet-on-wet, lay down a lighter and a darker cadmium-yellow wash. Leave a blank space between the three layers of the latte. Use a pink-powdered-sugar mixture for the cream and a cream-colored wash for the milk.

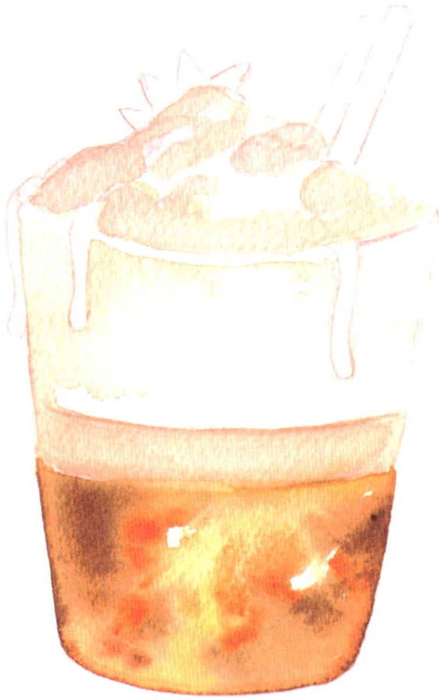

3 Working wet-on-wet, blend in a caramel ochre, a cadmium orange, and a few drops of burnt sienna into the base layer. Let the yellow stand out and draw attention to the dark areas. Use pink powdered sugar to paint the shadows of the cream.

4 Finish the cream with drops of burnt sienna. Lift off paint along the left side of the glass to mark its shadow. Paint the caramel sauce, cinnamon stick, and star anise. Lay down a first wash for the shadow cast by the glass.

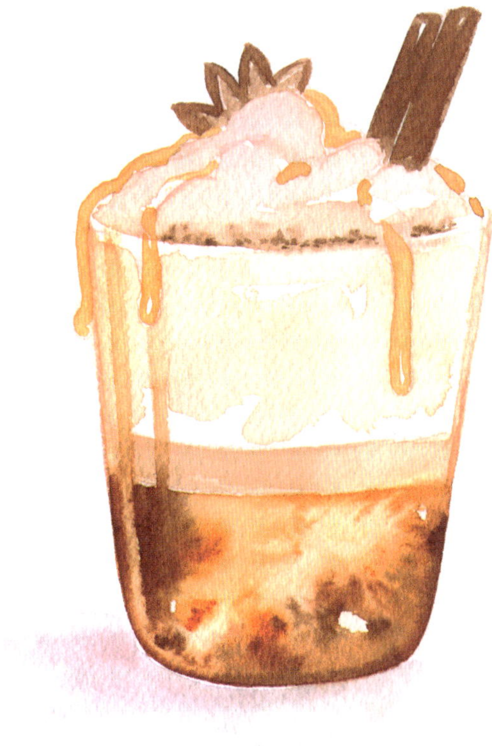

5 Paint little dots for the cacao powder, draw shadows on the caramel, and add light reflections. Finally, splash very fine splatters onto the latte to suggest vanilla. It's ready to serve!

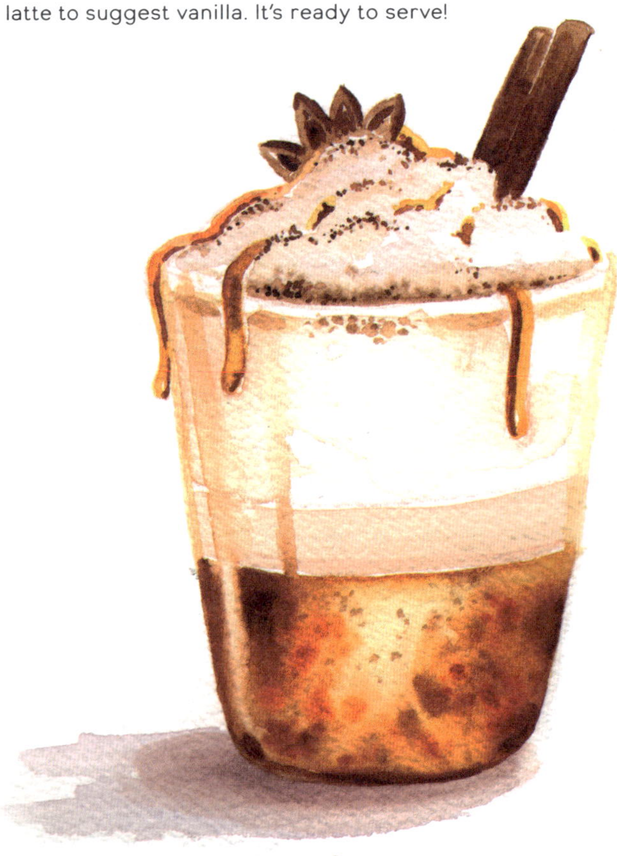

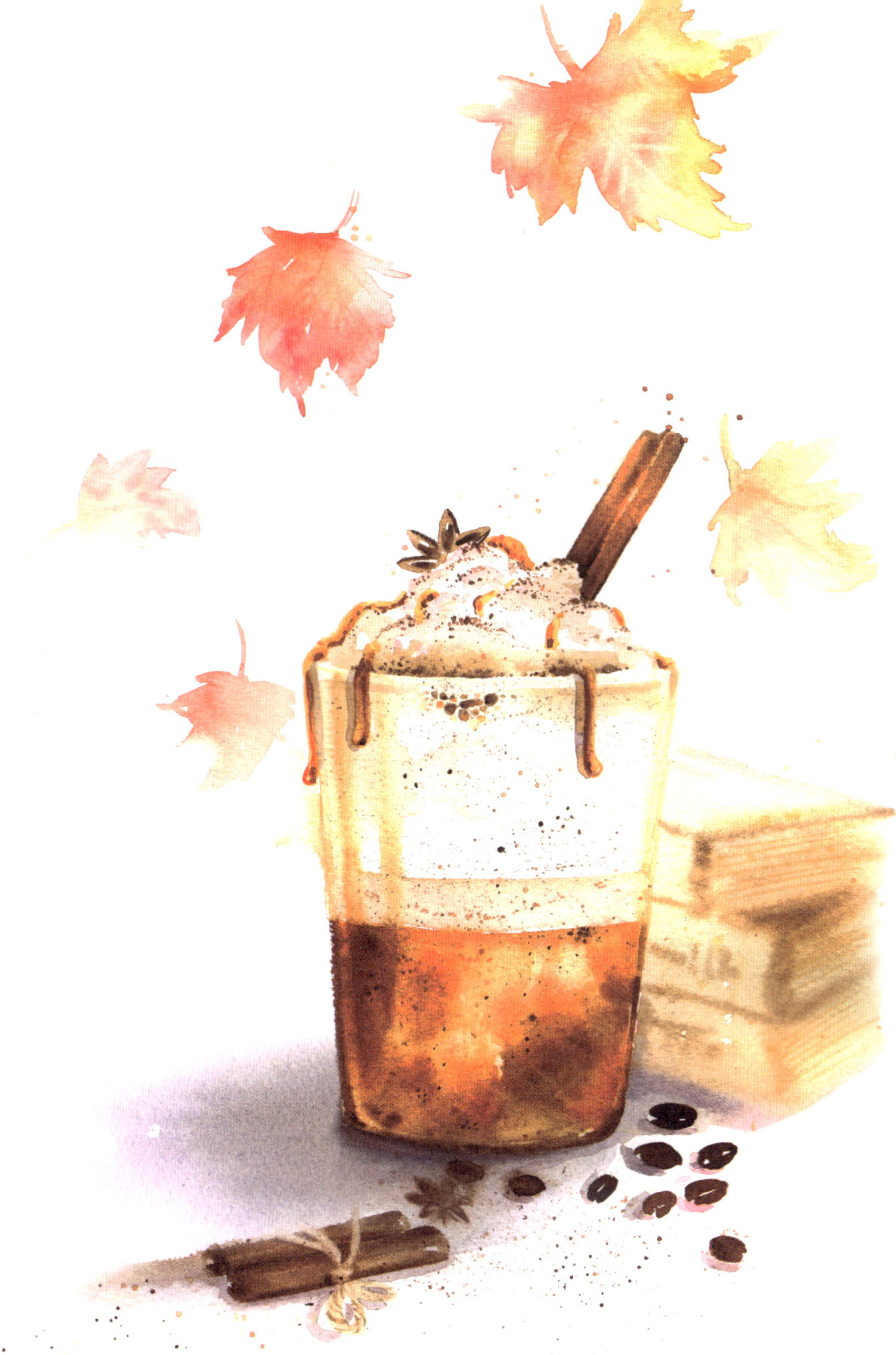

HALLOWEEN VIBES

Inspiration

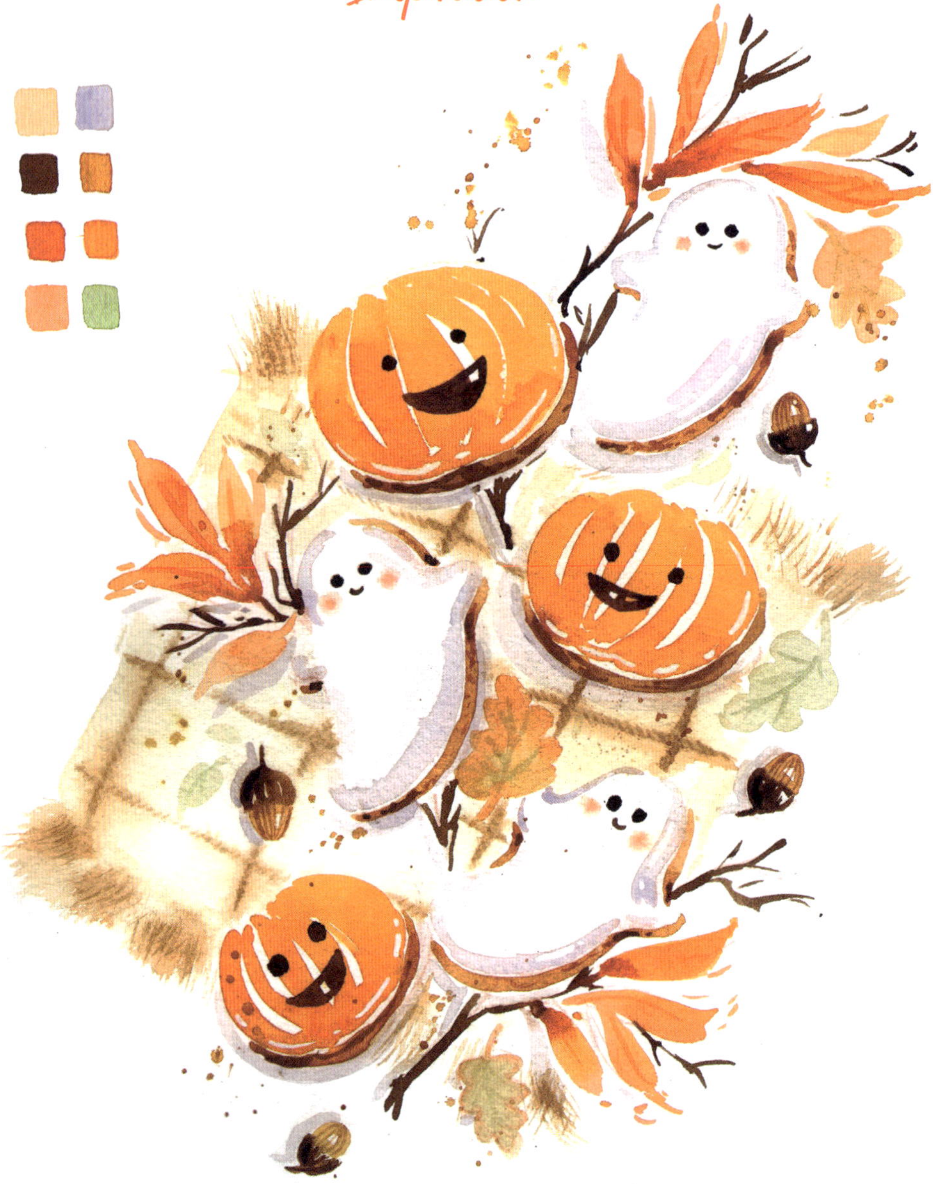

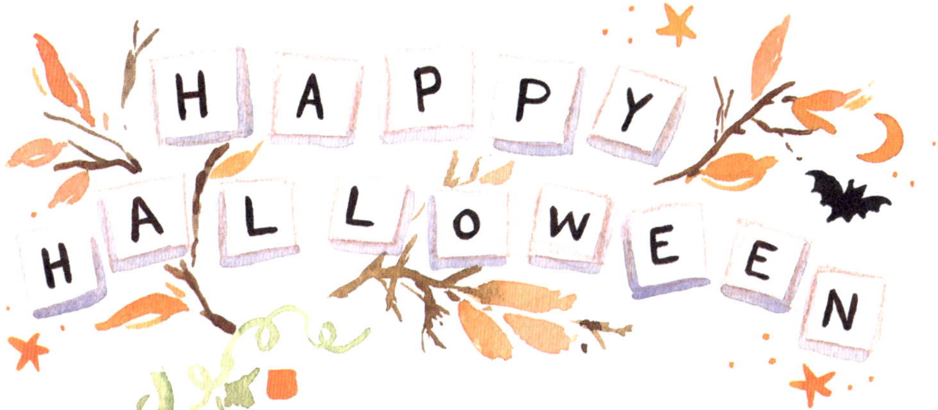

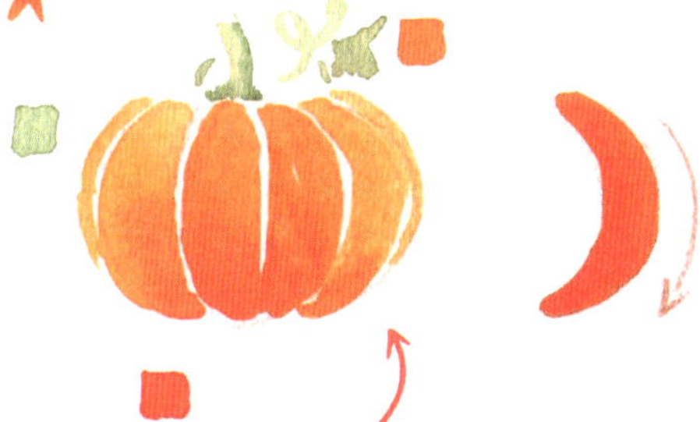

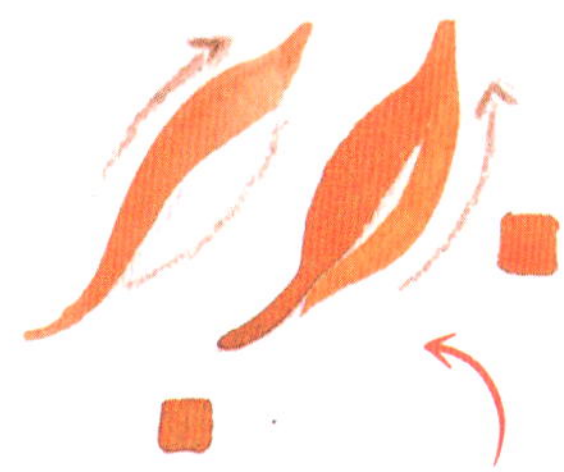

Use a synthetic round brush to make the clean curves of the pumpkin.

Play around with the pressure you apply to the brush. Use two colors and let them merge at the ends.

This design is all about the shadow!

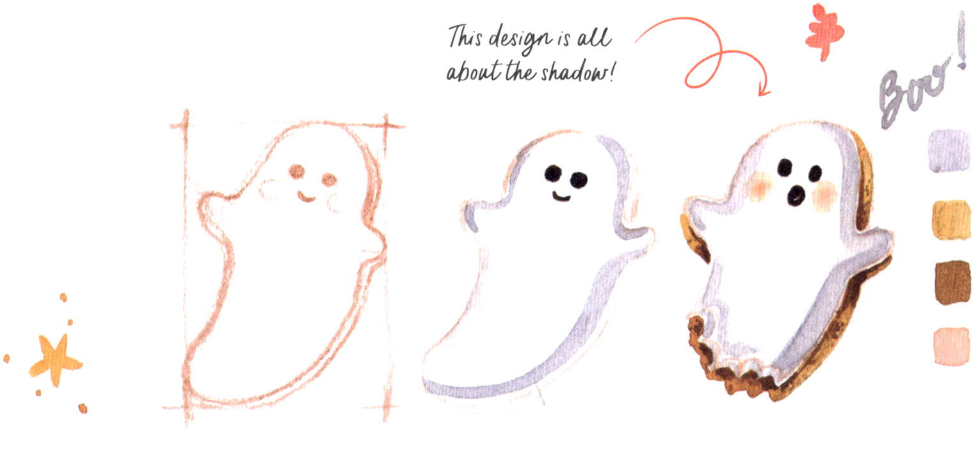

CHOCOLATE-CHIP COOKIES

Step by Step

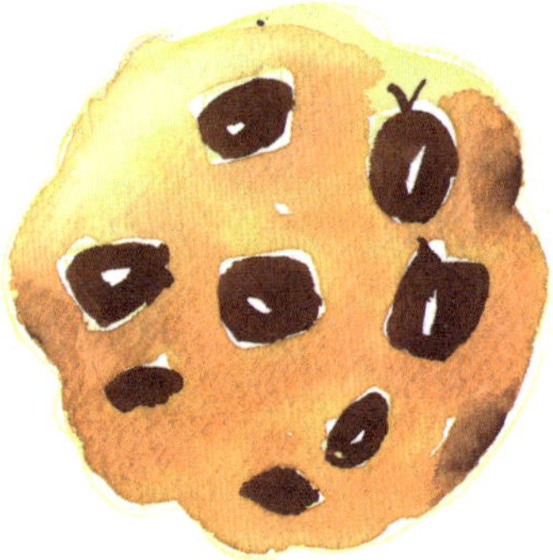

1 Using erasable pencils in yellow and brown, draw an irregular circle. Lay down a yellow wash, leaving some blank spaces for the chocolate chips. Fill these in with a mixture of brown shades, but preserve a very thin blank space around them to prevent the colors from blending.

2 Working wet-on-wet, apply an even layer of bold ochre with light but irregular brushstrokes. Add light reflections by lifting off paint with a dry brush. To depict the shadow, paint diluted shades of gray curving around the cookie, diluting more as you paint farther away from the cookie.

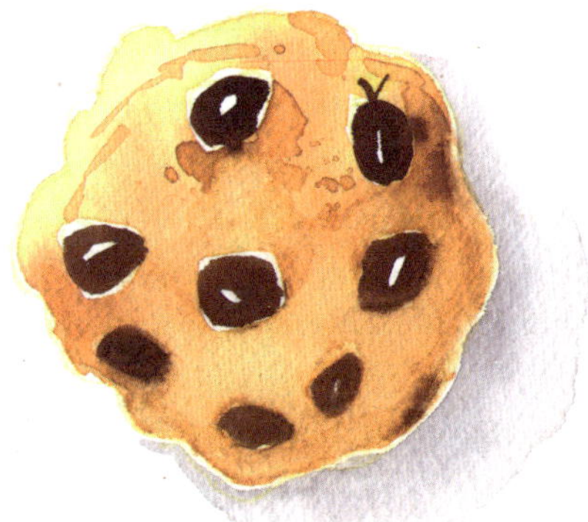

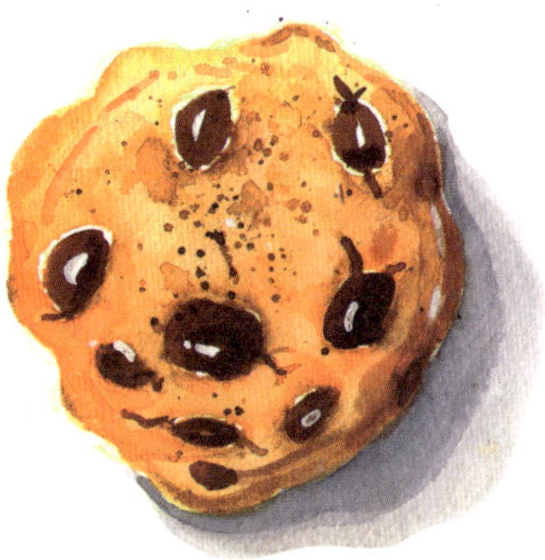

3 Working wet-on-wet, paint spots in different shades of brown and ochre, and then repeat, this time working dry-on-dry. Draw fine lines for the cracks and highlight the shadow at the edge of the cookie.

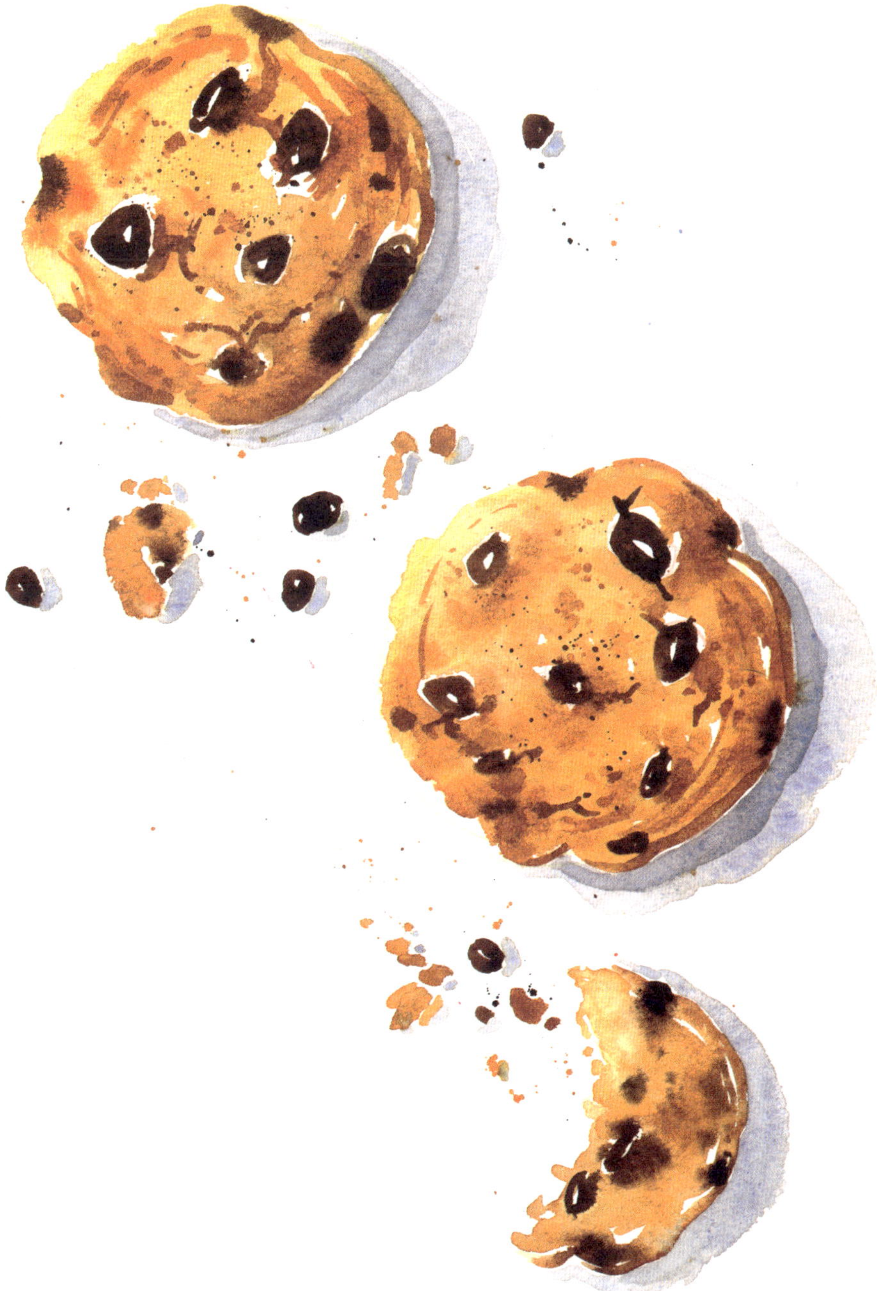

ÉCLAIRS

Step by Step

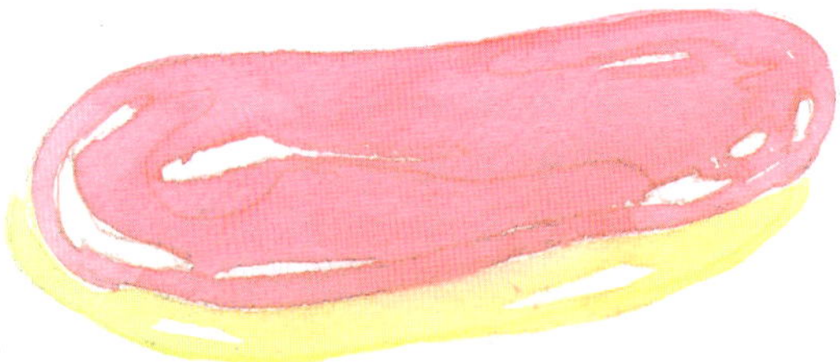

1 Paint the dough of the pastry in yellow and ochre. Leave a narrow blank gap between the dough and the icing to prevent the colors from blending together. Paint the icing in a diluted pink wash, giving it some light reflections (spaces left blank achieved with or without masking fluid).

2 Working wet-on-wet, make the edges of the icing darker with a bold pink-red paint mix. Working dry-on-dry, add ochre lines to give the doughy part of the pastry the impression of volume. Paint the shadow using a mixture of diluted cobalt blue and a hint of alizarin red.

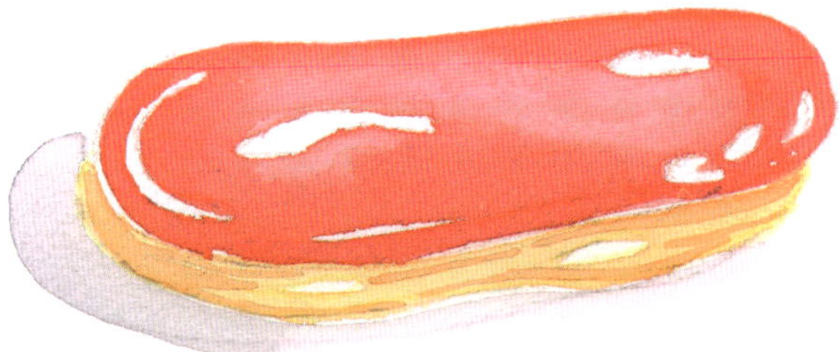

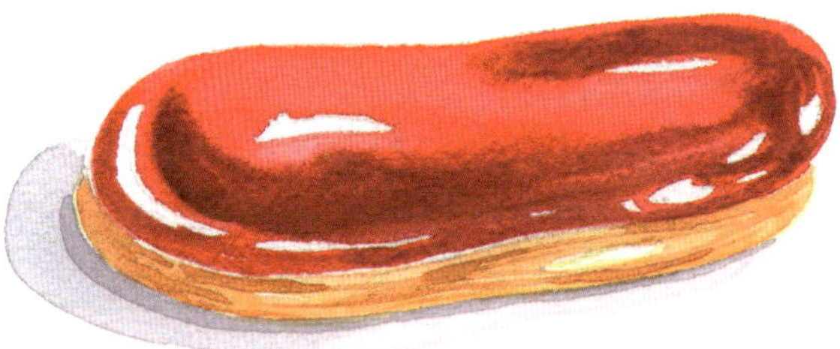

3 Working wet-on-wet, highlight the reflections of the icing with a dark-red paint. Working dry-on-dry, bring out the layers of the pastry with a highly pigmented ochre. Add a few more shadows around the edge of the éclair using a very diluted lavender pigment.

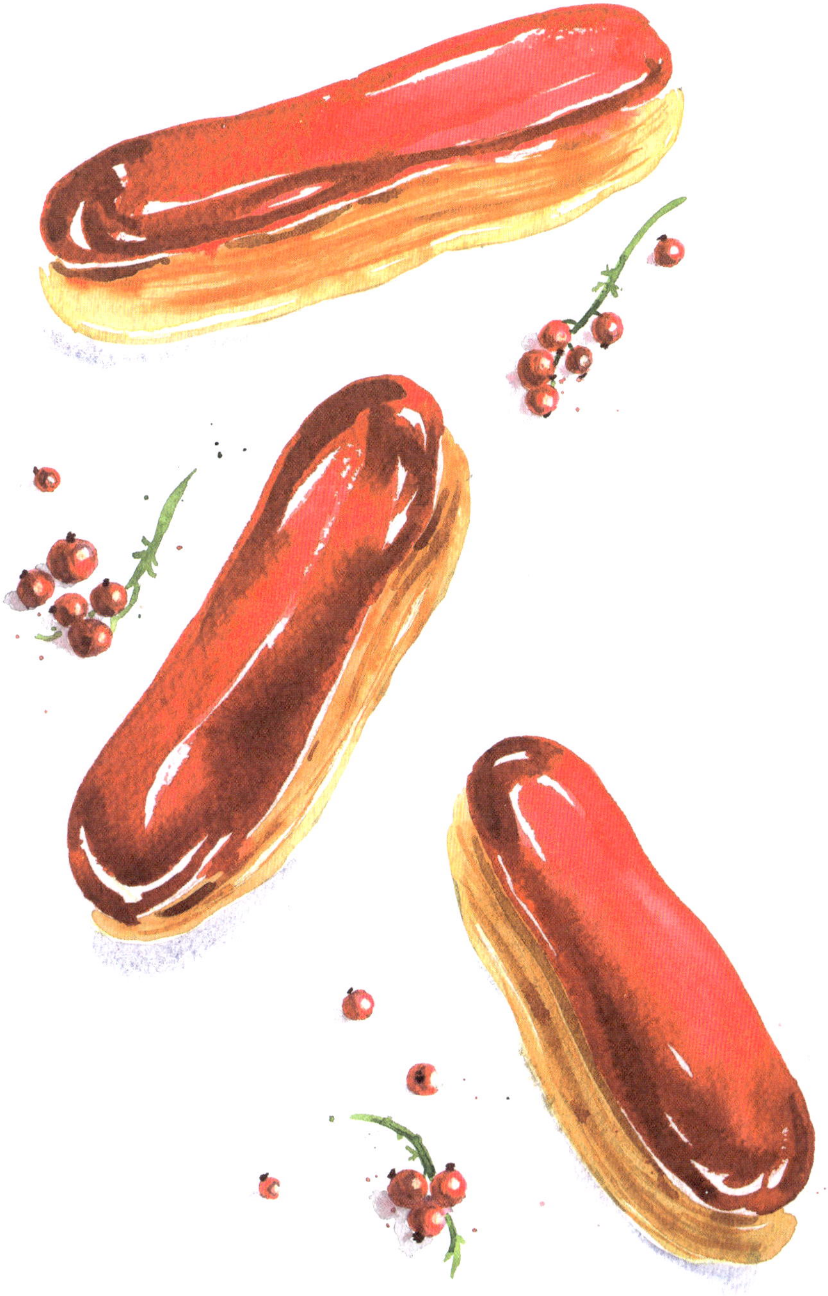

CHEESECAKE

Inspiration

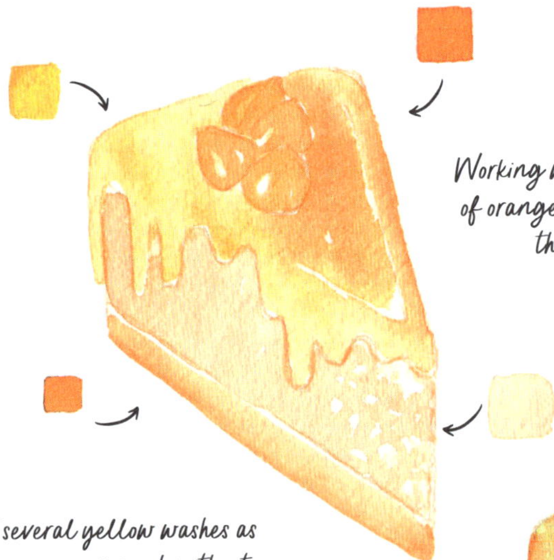

Working wet-on-wet, add a touch of orange ochre for the shadows of the caramel sauce.

Paint several yellow washes as well as a cream wash without blending them.

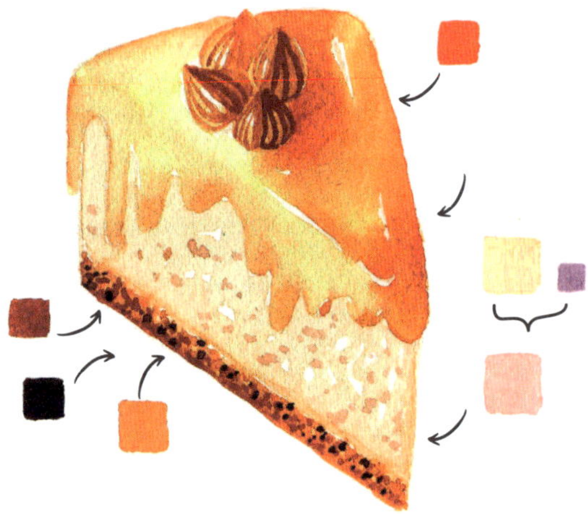

For the crunchy base of the cheesecake, paint several layers of dotted lines, working dry-on-dry (in burnt sienna, caramel, and chocolate).

With the tip of a fine brush and a mixture of cream and mauve, create the texture of the cream-cheese layer.

Add white highlights with a gel pen to make the cheesecake glisten. Bring out the shadows of the caramel further. If necessary, slightly rewet the area to allow for blending. Working dry-on-dry, paint a dark-brown shadow.

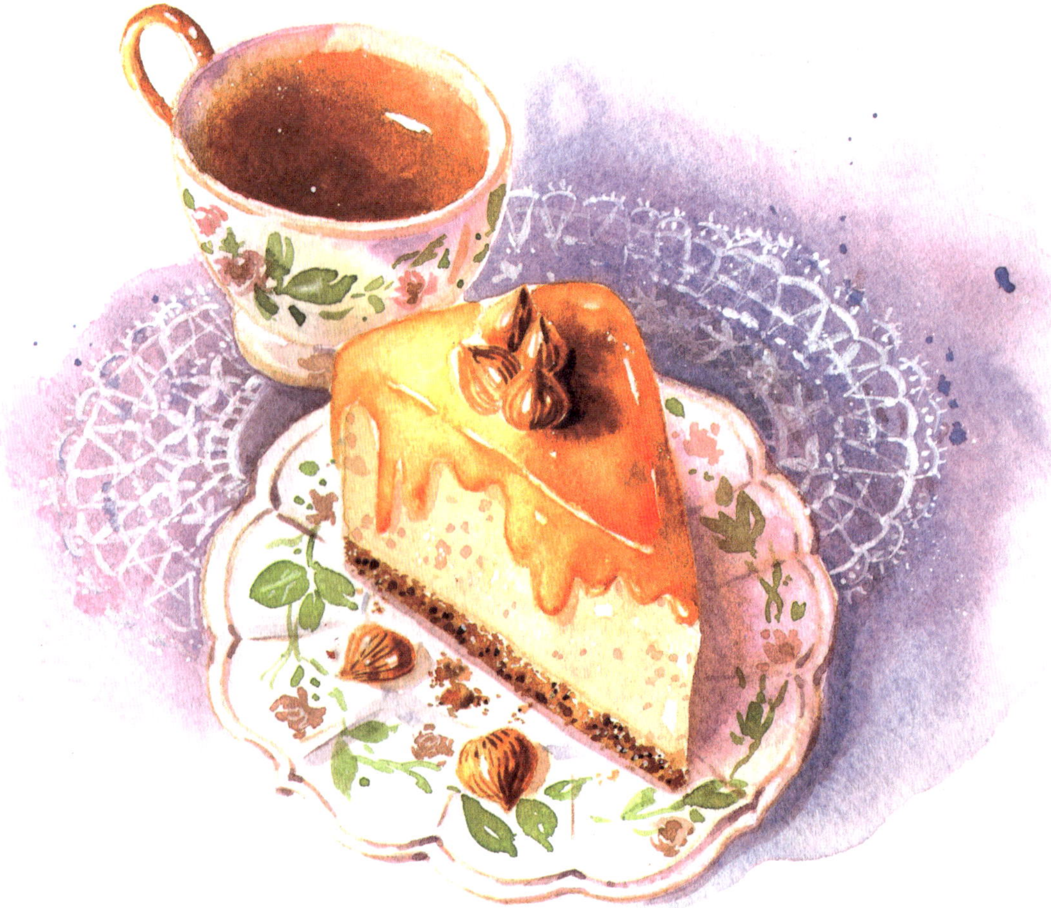

MADELEINES

Step by Step

1 Sketch a madeleine, including its grooves.

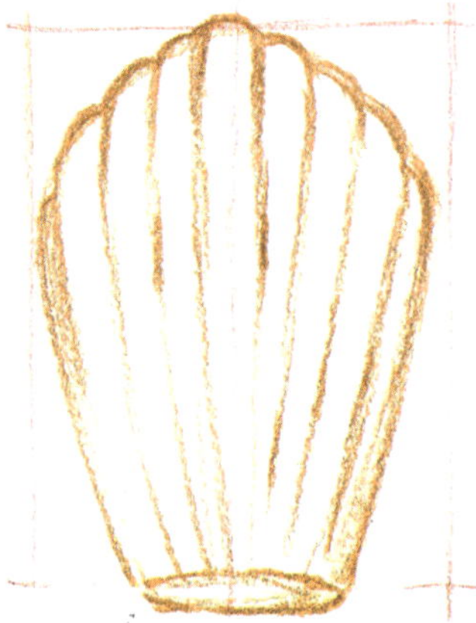

2 Working wet-on-wet, lay down a light cadmium-yellow wash, making brushstrokes from top to bottom using a round brush. Leave slivers of blank space between each groove.

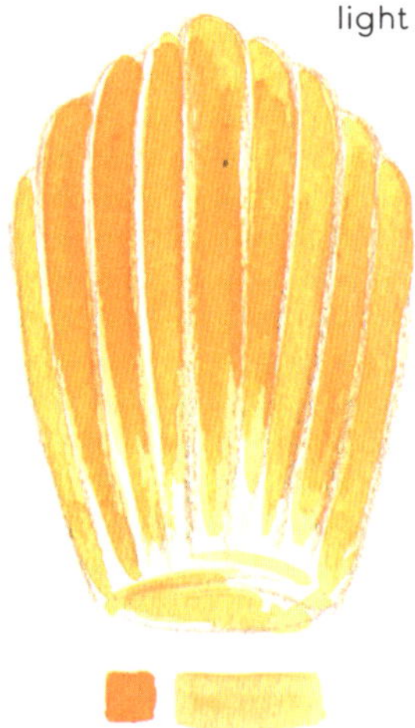

3 Working wet-on-wet, bring out the shadows with a bolder ochre caramel. Work across the madeleine without entirely covering the first layer. If necessary, remove a little watercolor from the wider sections. Working dry-on-dry, paint the rounded edges.

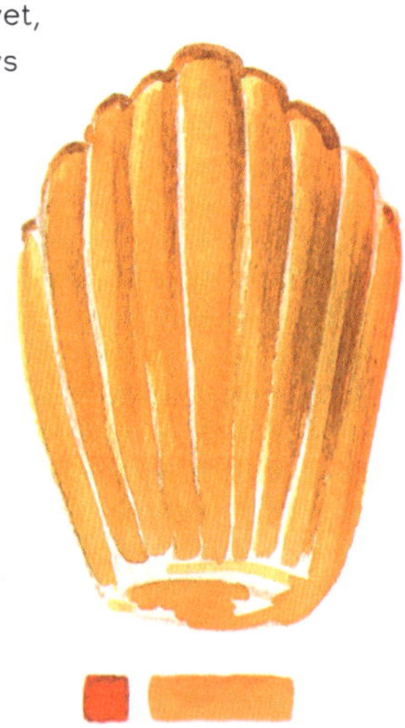

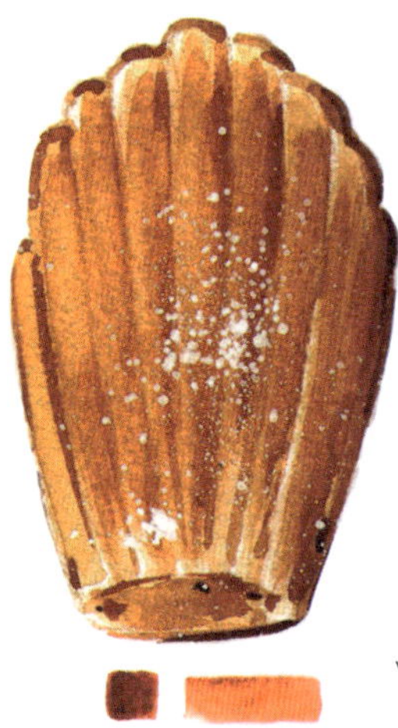

4 Still working dry-on-dry and using the tip of the brush, bring out some of the shadows further. For the powdered sugar, add splatters with white acrylic paint.

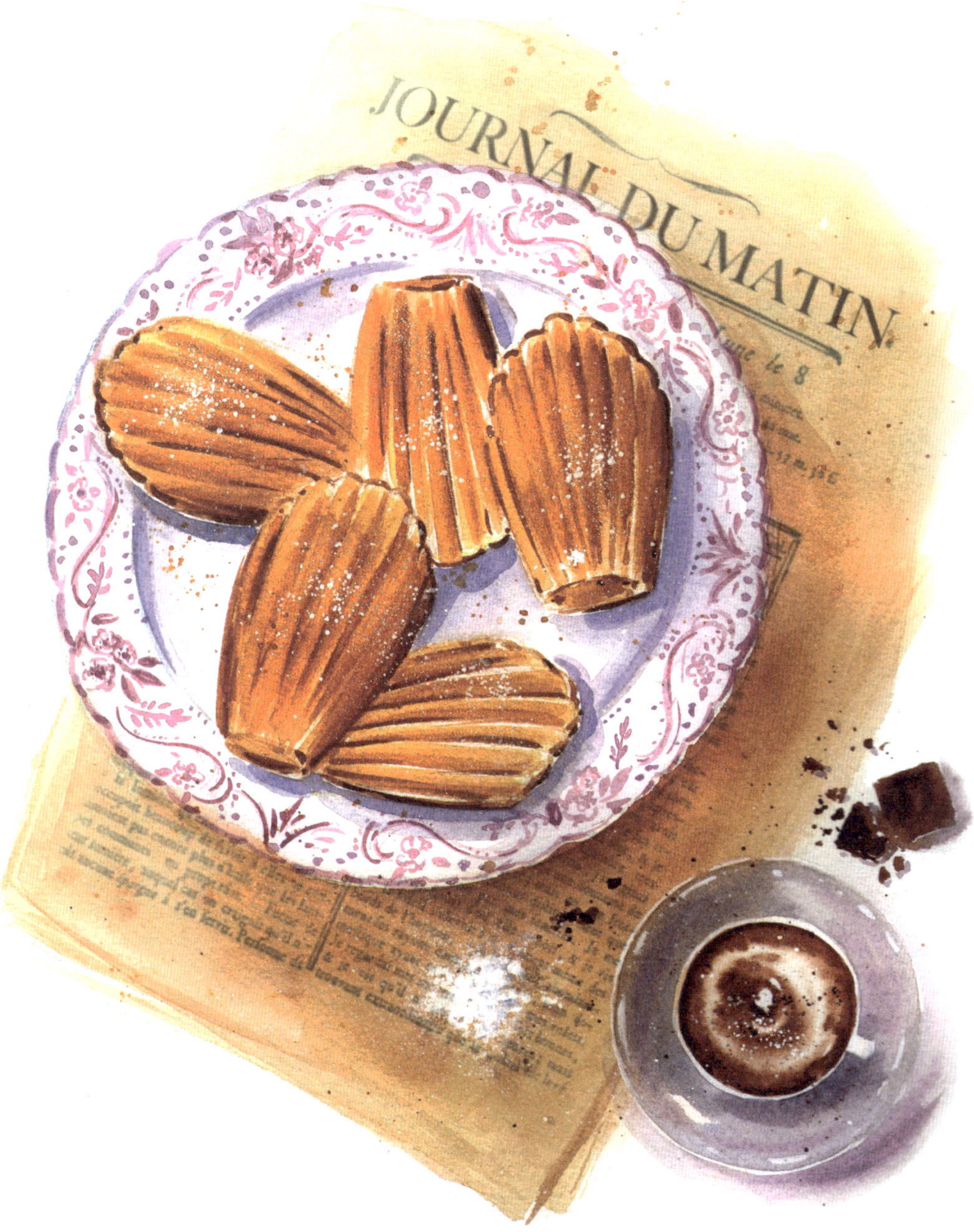
JOURNAL DU MATIN

WINTER TREATS

Inspiration

THE MAGIC OF THE HOLIDAYS AND A SNOWY LANDSCAPE OFFER SWEET INSPIRATION AND COZY DELIGHTS DURING THE COLD OF WINTER.

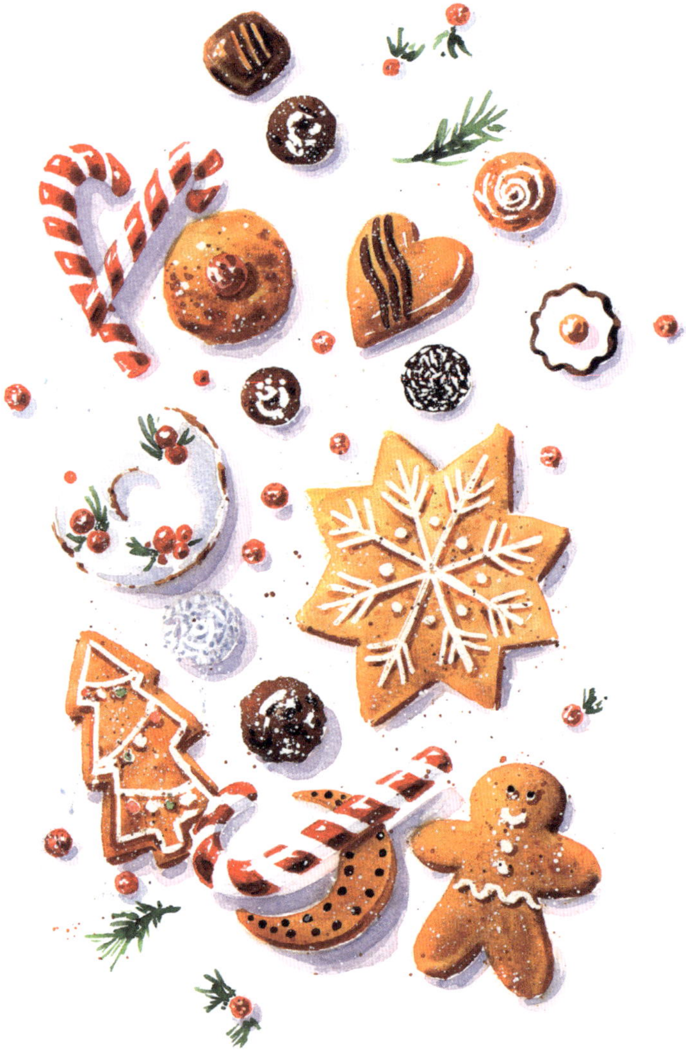

Begin by creating blank spaces using masking fluid. Remember: To protect your brush, dip it in soap (see page 36).

Bring out the shadow with a very diluted cobalt-blue wash and play around with the white background of the paper.

Leave blank space where the light would fall.

Lavender

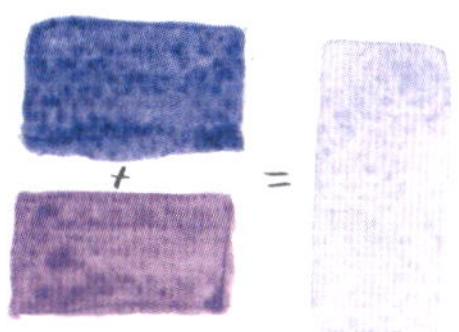

Wisteria

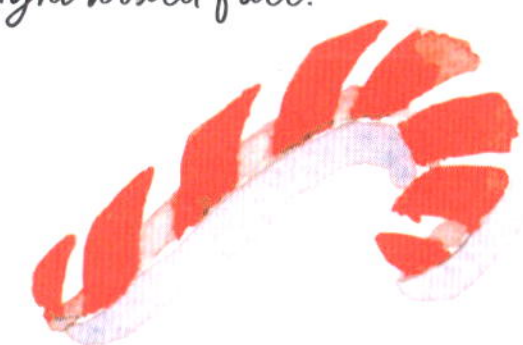

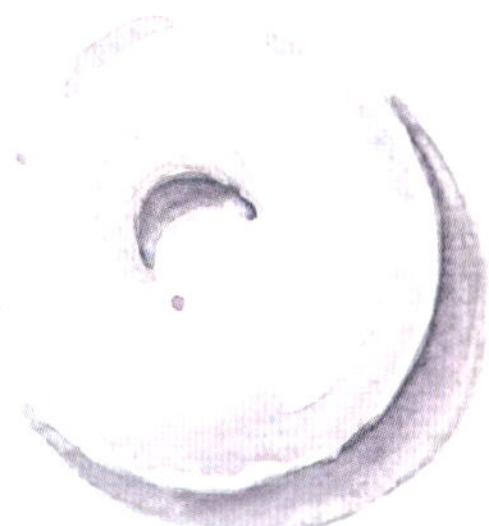

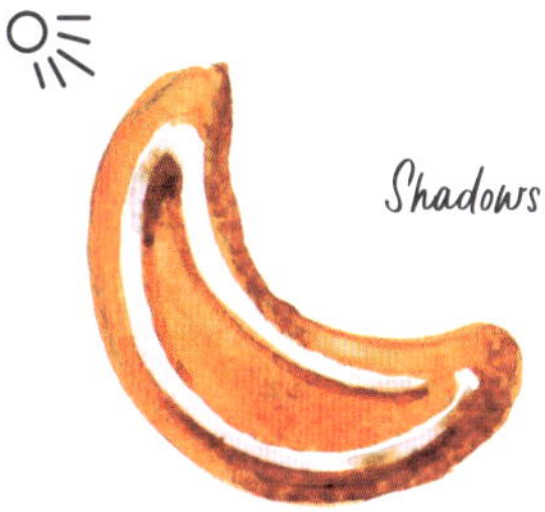

Shadows

The shadows fall on the right if the light comes from the left.

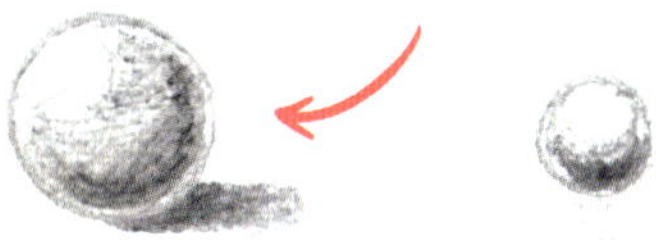

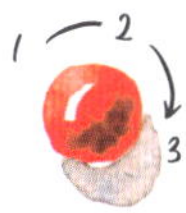

Vermilion red
+
Ochre and red
+
Alizarin red

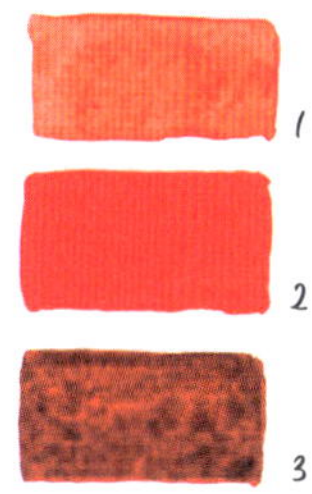

To portray your subject with the most convincing illusion of light, think about the different values of its main color. You need at least three values to create the effect of light reflecting on a three-dimensional object—its main color, a darker value, and a lighter value.

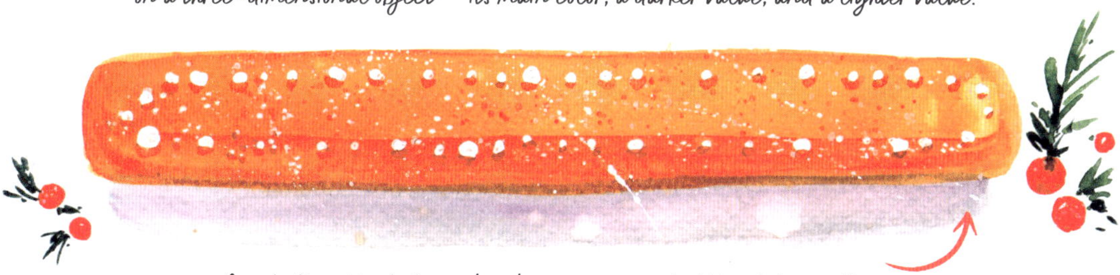

Create the effect of powdered sugar using a toothbrush to splatter or a fine-tipped paintbrush and a white paint marker.

GINGERBREAD MAN

Step by Step

THE ICONIC GINGERBREAD MAN! THESE COOKIES DATE BACK TO ELIZABETH I, WHO WANTED TO GIFT HER GUESTS OF HONOR COOKIES THAT LOOKED JUST LIKE THEM.

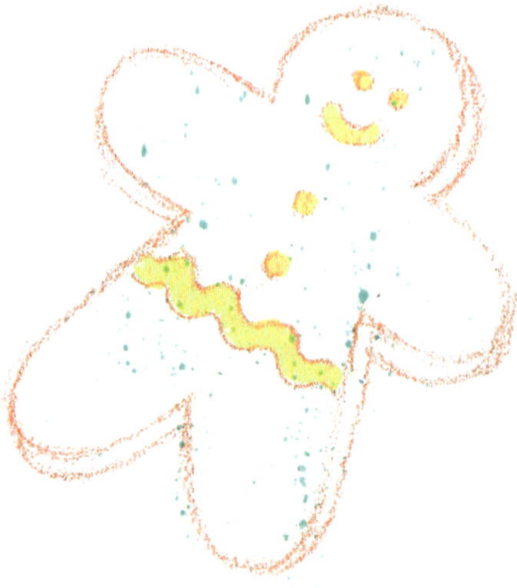

1 Sketch the cookie. Then, using masking fluid, block out blank spaces for the icing belt, buttons, mouth, and eyes.

2 Working wet-on-wet, lay down a yellow-ochre wash.

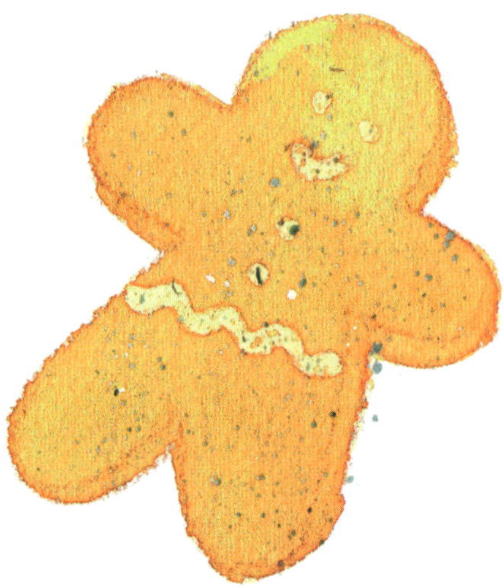

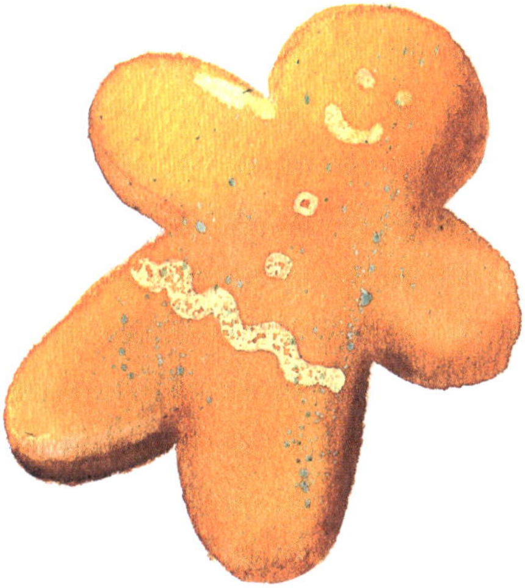

3 Working wet-on-wet, make the shadows darker with a mixture of bold brown. Create texture by adding a darker shade to the body of the gingerbread man as well.

4 Working dry-on-dry, sprinkle the cookie with spots in different shades of brown and ochre. With a more-diluted paint, draw the shadow of the icing, then add the drop shadow in mauve gray. Remove the masking fluid, bring out the shadows, and add some detail to the eyes and smile.

CHRISTMAS PUDDING

Step by Step

IN MY FAMILY, MY FATHER PASSED DOWN THE TRADITION OF THE CHRISTMAS PUDDING. HE TOLD US HOW MY GRANDMOTHER USED TO MAKE IT WITH STALE BREAD AND CANDIED FRUIT. IT'S SERVED FLAMBÉED WITH RUM AND A BIG DOLLOP OF CREAMY CUSTARD. WHAT A DELIGHT!

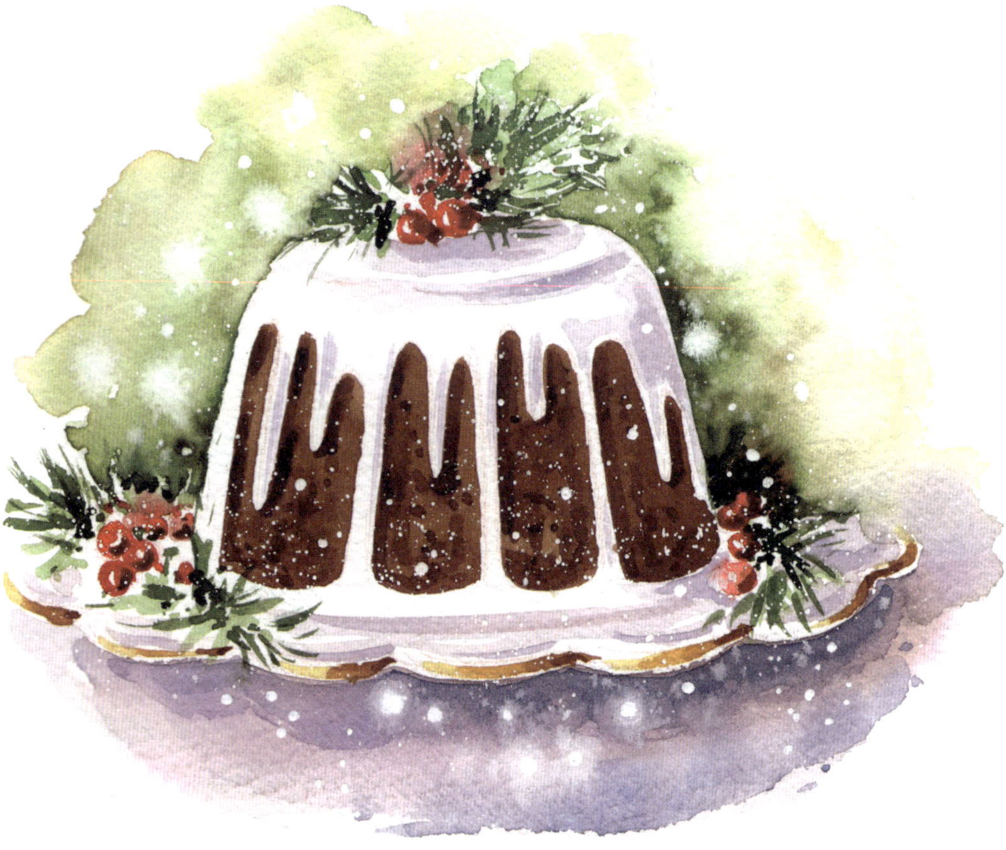

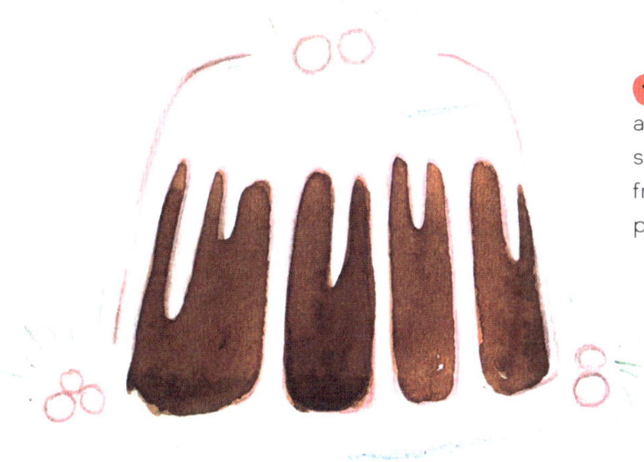

1 After making a sketch, lay down a light-chocolate wash, reserving some blank spaces for the sections of frosting and making certain areas of paint darker.

2 Paint the shadows of the cream with a mauve-gray paint mix. Paint the fruit and a few darker spots in the chocolate red to add texture and volume.

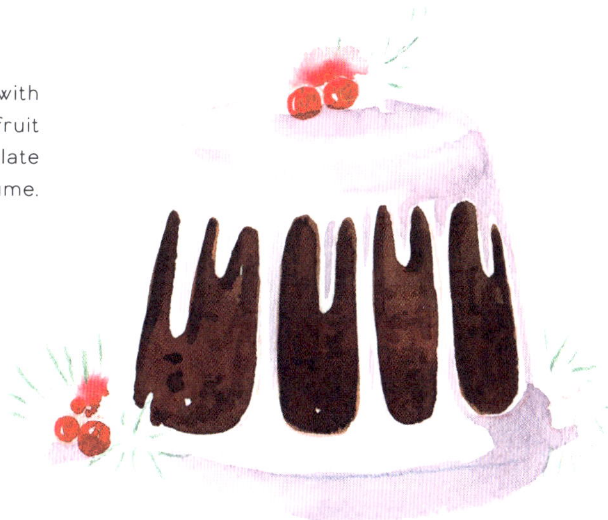

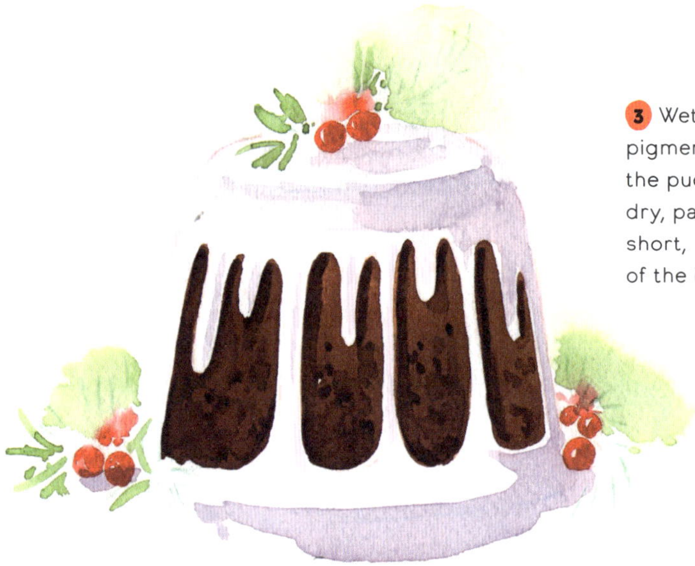

3 Wet the backdrop. Add diluted green pigment in decorative splotches around the pudding. In the sections that are dry, paint some pine needles using short, precise lines. Paint the shadows of the icing in chocolate brown.

4 Still working wet-on-wet, add hints of yellow green, sap green, and dark green to the background. Paint the shadows of the red fruit. Working dry-on-dry, add white-acrylic splatters to the chocolate; working wet-on-wet, add white-acrylic splatters to the backdrop. This is sure to add a magical effect!

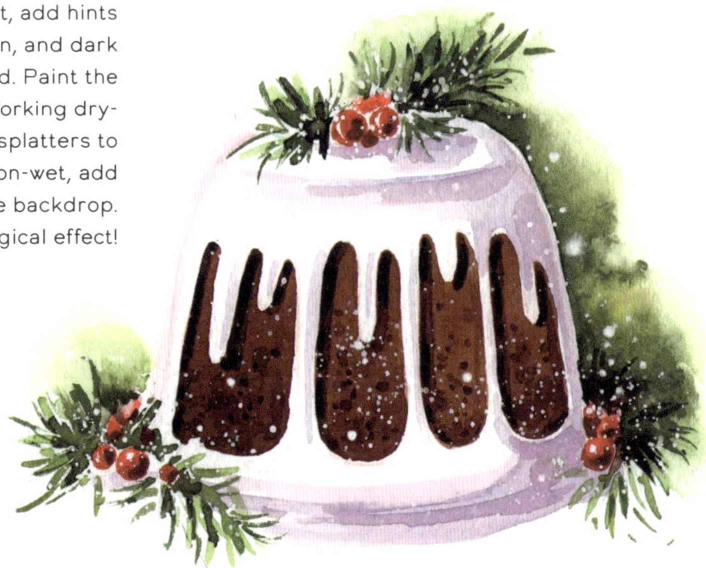

CANDY CANES

Step by Step

CANDY CANES ARE THE EPITOME OF CHRISTMAS MAGIC! I JUST LOVE TO SEE THEM DANGLING FROM THE CHRISTMAS TREE WITH ALL THE OTHER CHARMING DECORATIONS.

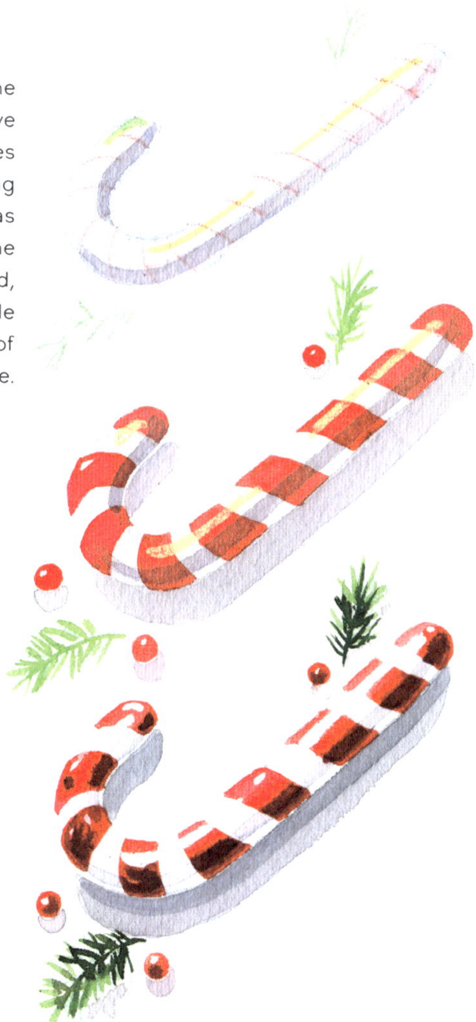

1 Lightly sketch the candy cane and reserve areas for bright sparkles of light using masking fluid (which shows as yellow here). Once the masking fluid has dried, paint the shadows inside with a diluted mixture of blue and purple.

2 Paint the red stripes and berries with a vermilion paint mix. Working dry-on-dry, paint the drop shadows of the berries and the candy cane. Paint the sprigs in moss green.

3 Accentuate the hues with red and green. Bring out the shadows along the edge of the candy cane with a darker paint mix. Once the work has dried, remove the masking fluid.

ASSORTED CHOCOLATES

Step by Step

A CLASSIC BOX OF CHRISTMAS CHOCOLATES! THEY SAY THAT HAPPINESS AWAITS WHERE YOU LEAST EXPECT IT. WHILE THAT MAY BE TRUE, CHOCOLATES IN ALL THEIR SHAPES AND FLAVORS MAKE ME HAPPY WITHOUT FAIL.

1 With masking fluid (shown in yellow here), paint the blank spaces and the bits of shredded coconut. Lay down an orange-ochre wash for the chocolate truffle and moss-green wash for the matcha truffle (at bottom).

2 Accentuate the colors: Use red brown (for the first chocolate and the third flower-shaped chocolate), orange ochre (for the center of the flower-shaped chocolate), mauve gray (for the shadows of the shredded coconut), and sap green (for the shadows of the matcha truffle). Paint all the drop shadows with a diluted mauve-gray paint mix.

3 Add a couple splatters of color to the first chocolate. Once your artwork is dry, remove the masking fluid and accentuate the shadows further. If you're up to it, try re-creating the other chocolates on the right-hand page as well!

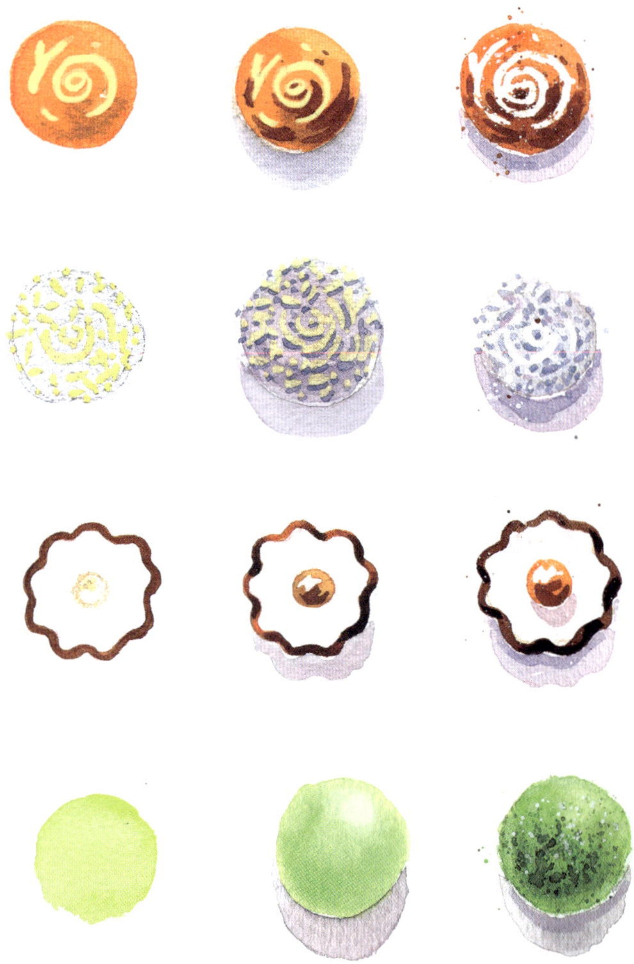

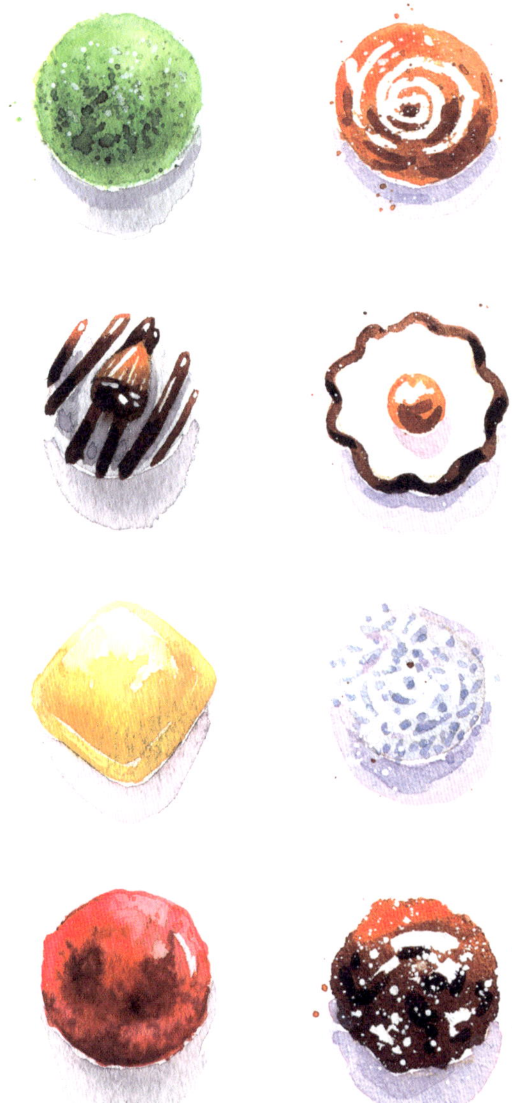

HOT COCOA

Step by Step

WHO CAN RESIST A WARM MUG OF RICH HOT CHOCOLATE BY THE FIRESIDE? I LOVE THREADING MY MARSHMALLOWS ONTO A TOOTHPICK AND DIPPING THEM INTO THAT CUP OF DELICIOUSNESS!

1. Sketch the marshmallow with an erasable mauve pencil. Start with a rectangle, then sketch two ovals at the top and bottom.

2. Working wet-on-wet, lay down a mauve wash. Keep lighter areas clear by leaving the paper dry. If necessary, blend the contours with a clean, dry brush.

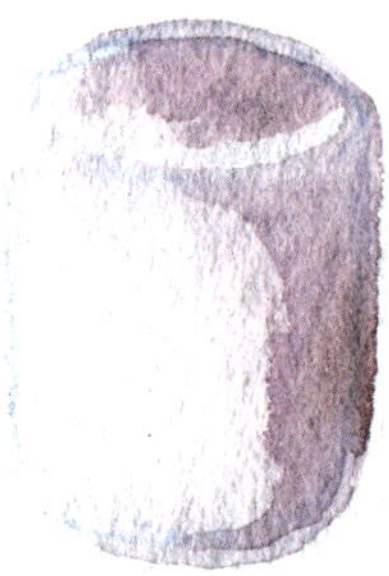

3. Working wet-on-wet, make the shaded areas darker with a bolder mixture of mauve by adding a touch of burnt sienna to it.

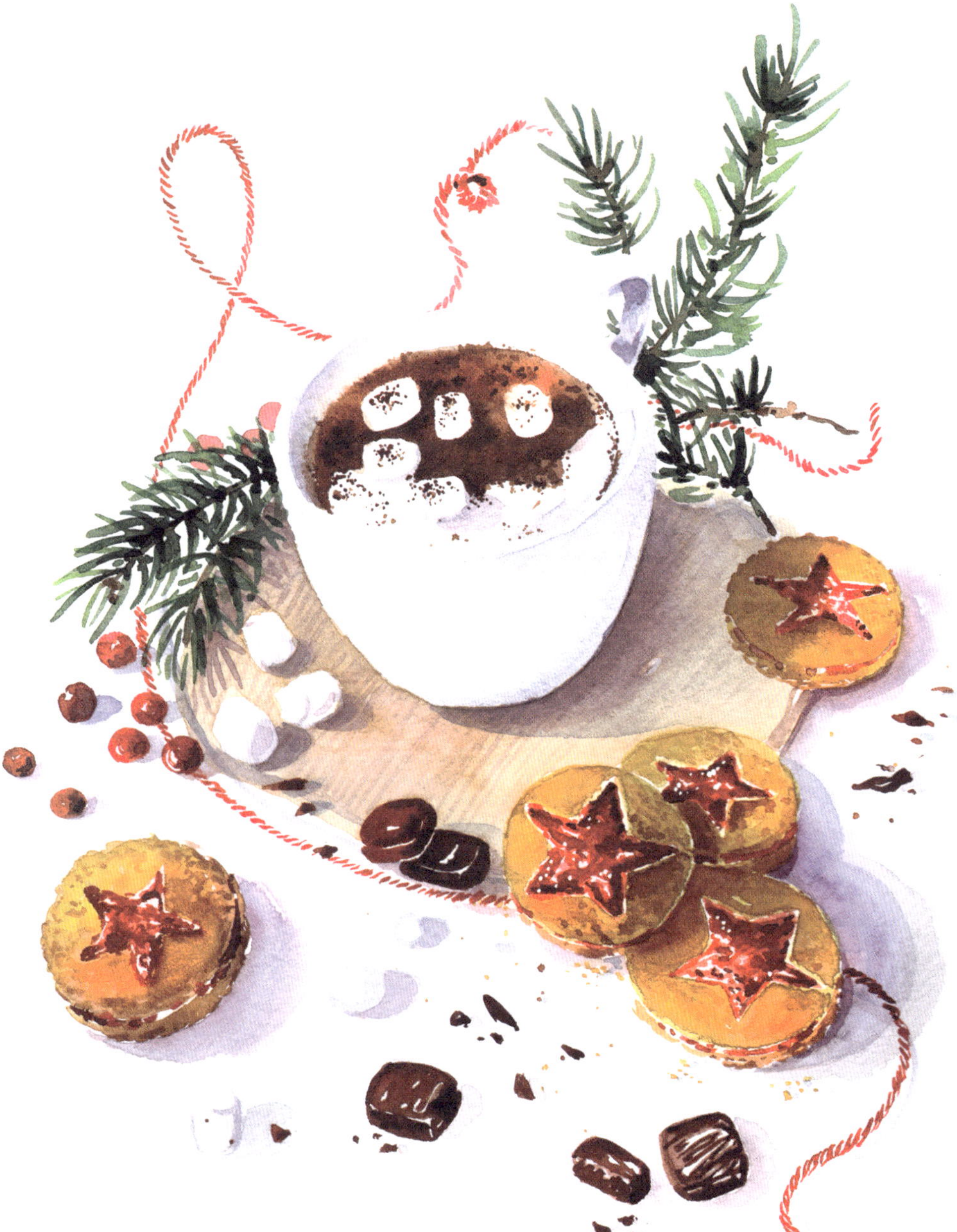

WAFFLES

Step by Step

1 Sketch the teaspoon with an erasable pencil. Lay down a mauve-gray wash inside the spoon part. Lift off color in the shape of an arc to create the effect of a curve within the spoon part. Lay down the same wash for the handle. Leave some blank space at the end of the handle for a glisten of light.

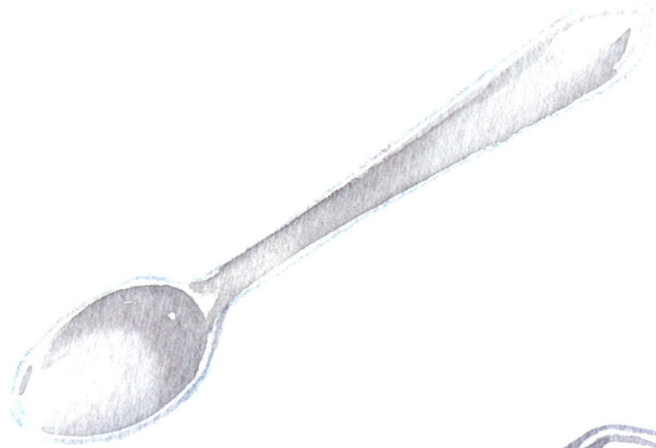

2 Working wet-on-wet, go back over all the areas you outlined in the previous step to deepen the pigment. Once this layer of paint has dried, trace the contours and edges of the spoon with a darker-mauve-gray paint mix.

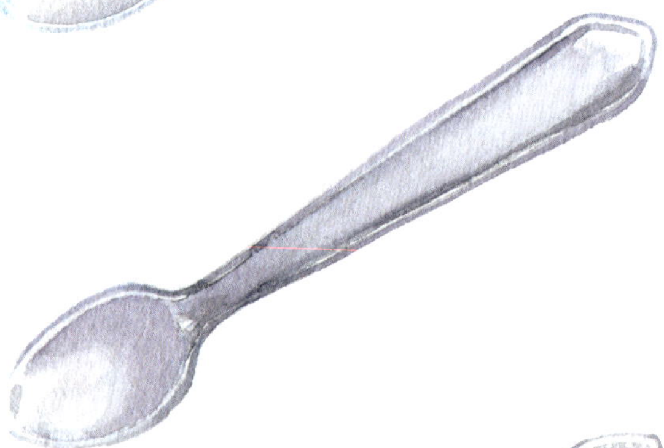

3 Bring out the shadow on the inside of the spoon. With a gel pen, draw small dots along the very edges of the handle to make it look more realistic and give it some texture.

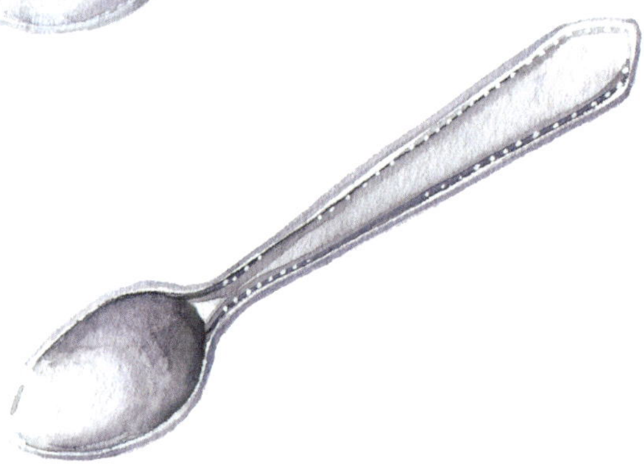

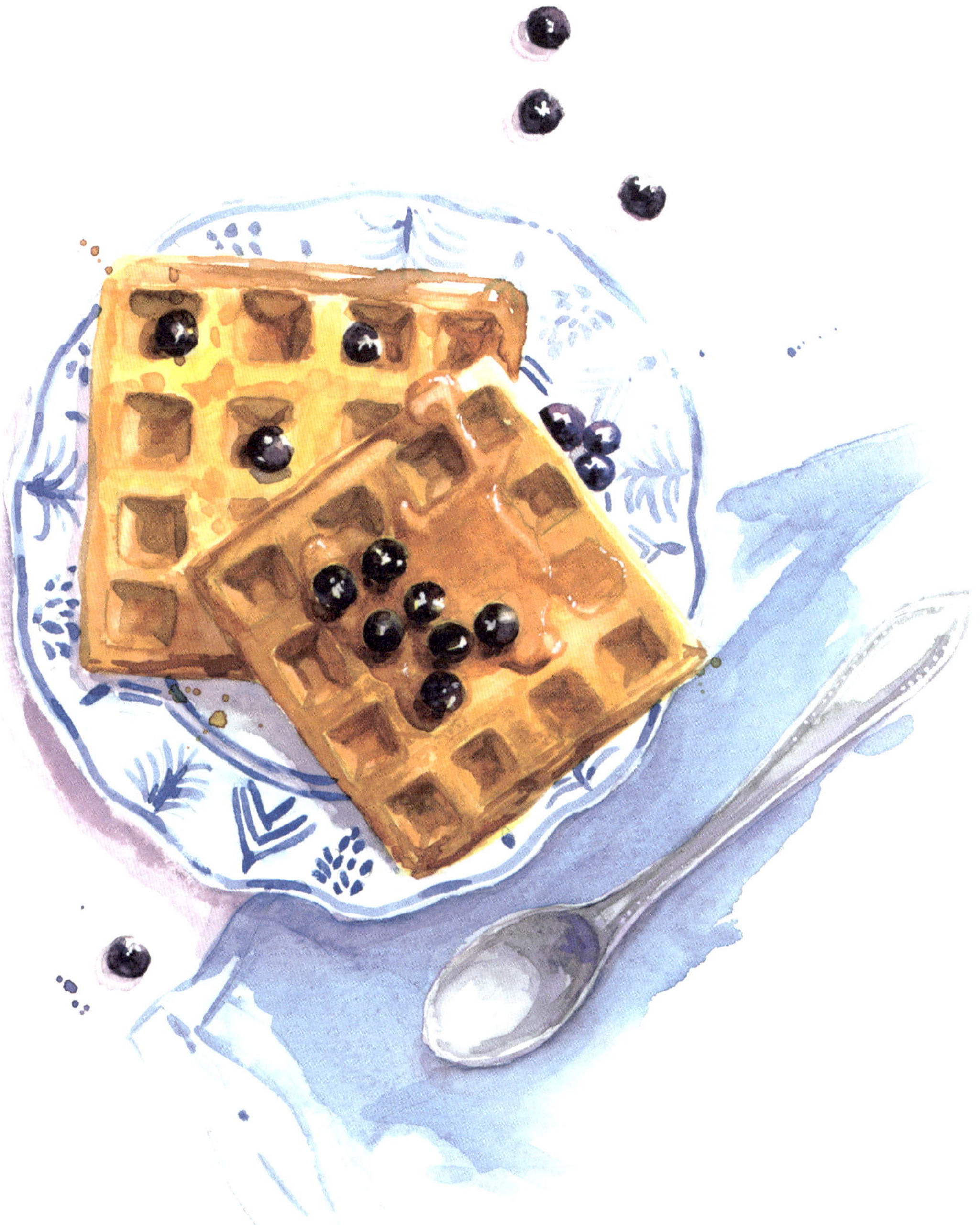

CRÊPES

Recipe

Make your sketches in a grid and use it to check the proportions of the various items.

"Farine" is flour!

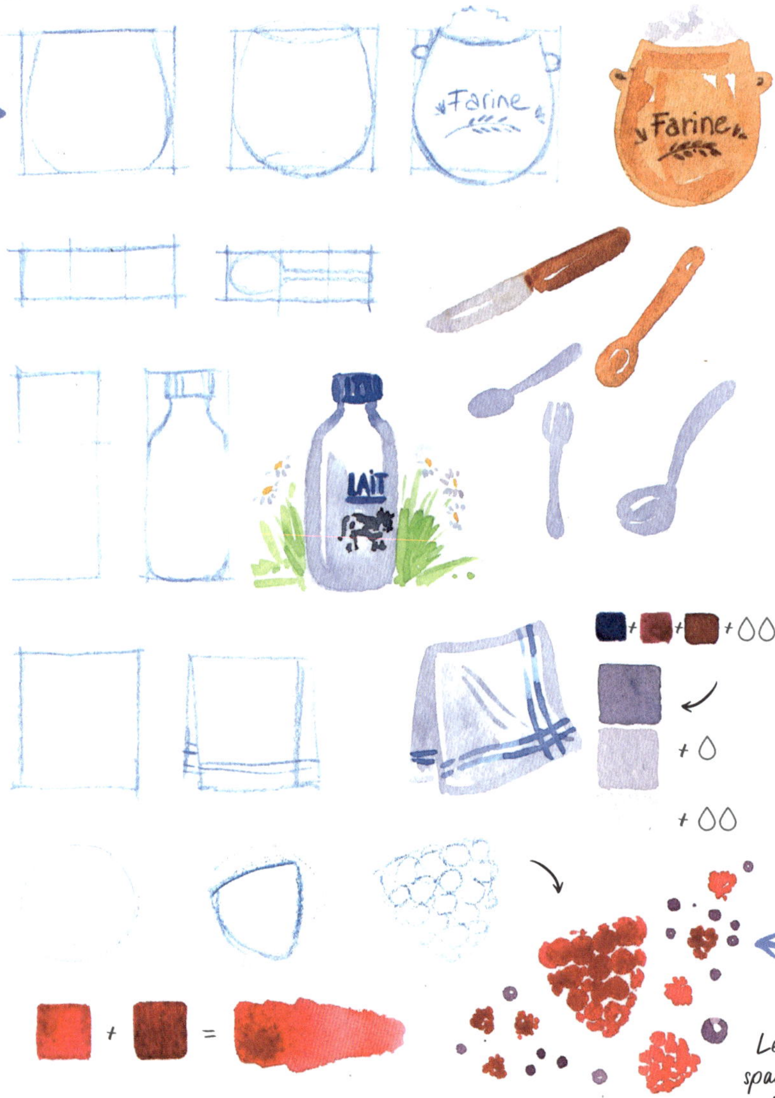

"Lait" is milk!

Leave blank spaces between each little berry segment.

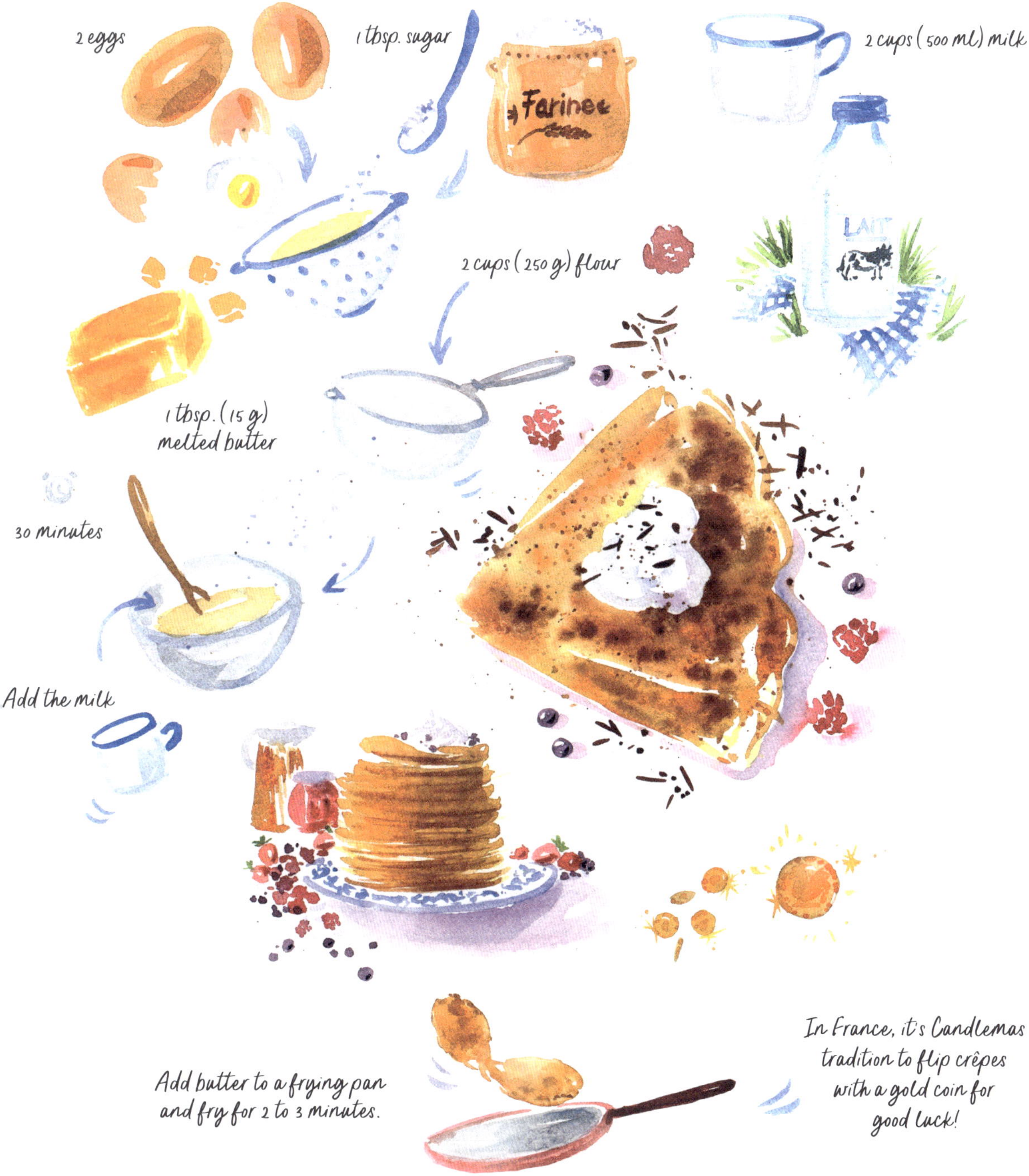
2 eggs
1 tbsp. sugar
Farine
2 cups (500 ml) milk
LAIT
2 cups (250 g) flour
1 tbsp. (15 g) melted butter
30 minutes
Add the milk
Add butter to a frying pan and fry for 2 to 3 minutes.
In France, it's Candlemas tradition to flip crêpes with a gold coin for good luck!

TEACUP

Inspiration

WHENEVER I WOULD VISIT MY GRANDMOTHER, SHE WOULD SERVE TEA FROM THESE PRETTY BLUE TEACUPS, WITH A TINY PITCHER FOR MILK ON THE SIDE. IT'S A TRULY FOND MEMORY OF MINE.

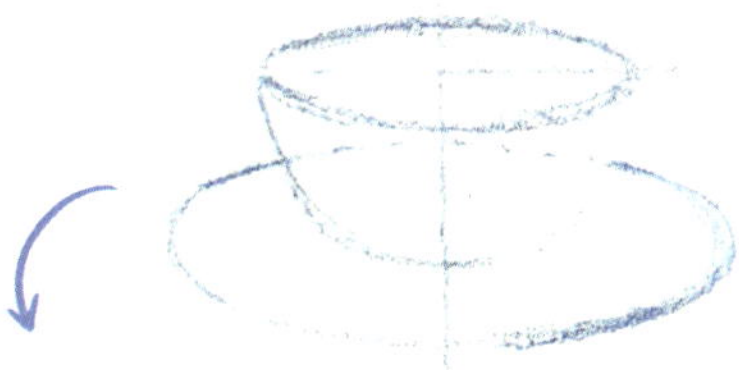

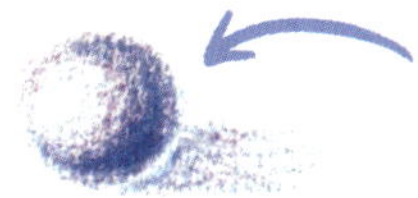

Make sure to decide where the light is coming from in your illustration! The shadow inside the cup will be on the opposite side from the cast shadow.

Sketching guidelines for symmetry can be very useful when drawing ovals.

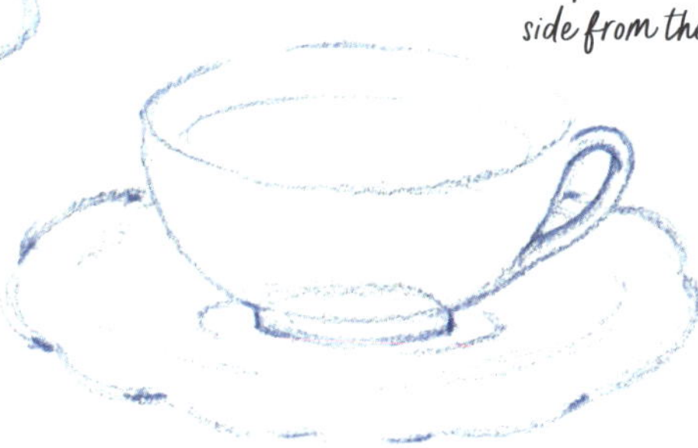

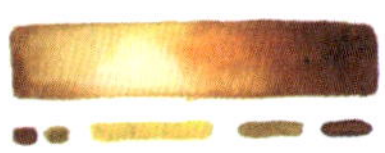

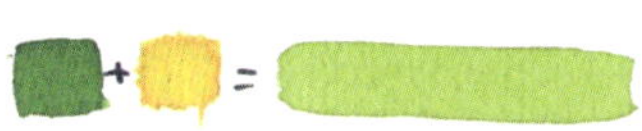

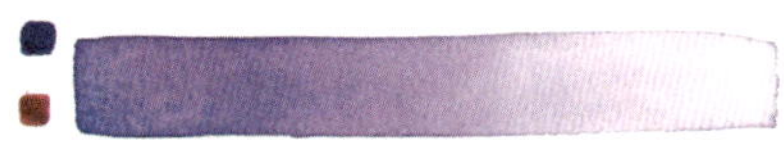

The tea, in its various shades, is painted working wet-on-wet.

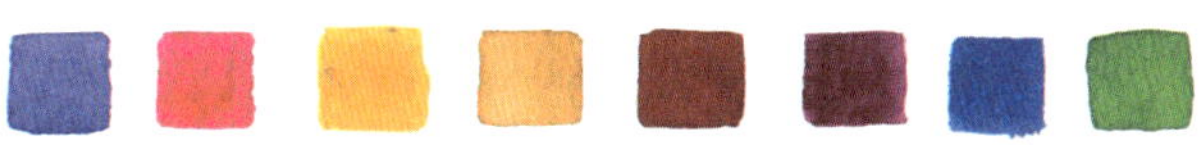

MACARONS

Step by Step

MACARONS ORIGINALLY COME FROM THE MIDDLE EAST. CATHERINE DE MÉDICIS INTRODUCED THEM TO FRANCE DURING THE RENAISSANCE. SINCE THEN, THEY HAVE CHANGED A GREAT DEAL: FROM PLAIN ALMOND BISCUITS TO A CRUNCHY MINI-CAKE WITH A MELT-IN-YOUR-MOUTH FILLING.

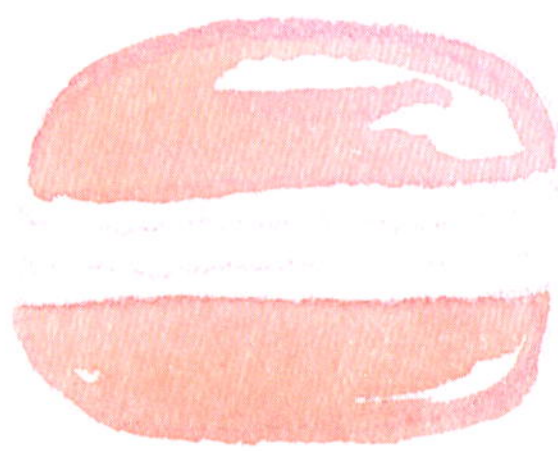

1 Sketch the macaron with an erasable pencil. Gently lighten the lines with a kneadable eraser. Lay down a coral-pink wash, leaving blank spaces for glistening light on the cookie.

2 Make the shadows stand out with a bolder paint mixture. Paint small spots for the frilled edges of the cookies and lay down a bright-pink wash at the center for the filling.

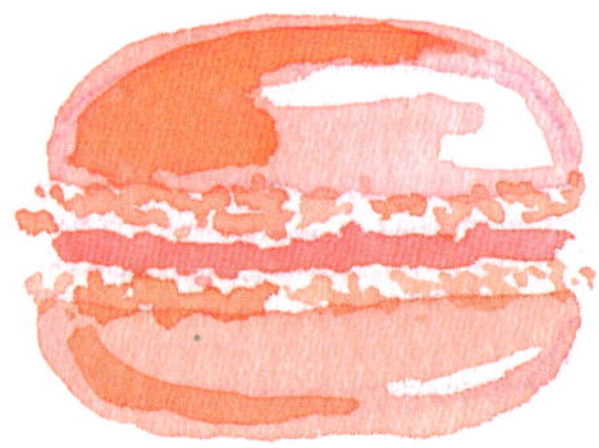

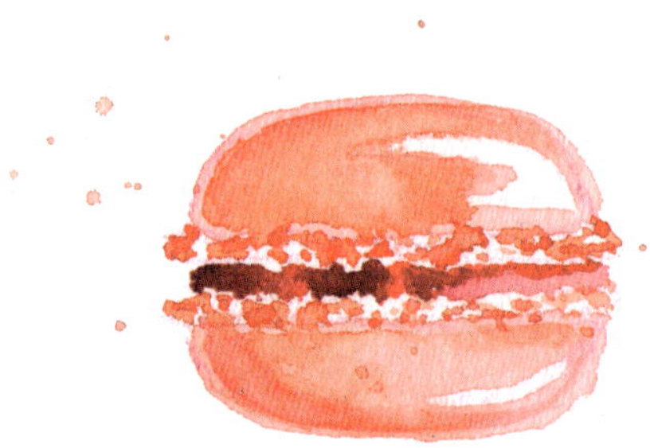

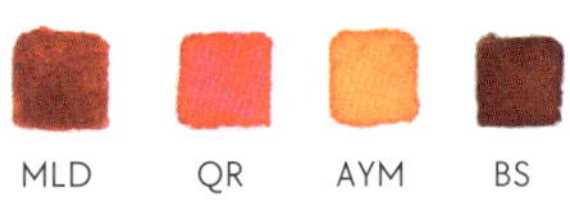

3 Make the shaded areas darker with a coral-pink paint mixture. Make the frilled edges stand out with a bolder paint mixture. Darken the filling with red and a touch of burnt sienna. Finish the painting by adding a few splatters with the first coral-pink mix. Your macaron is ready for snacking!

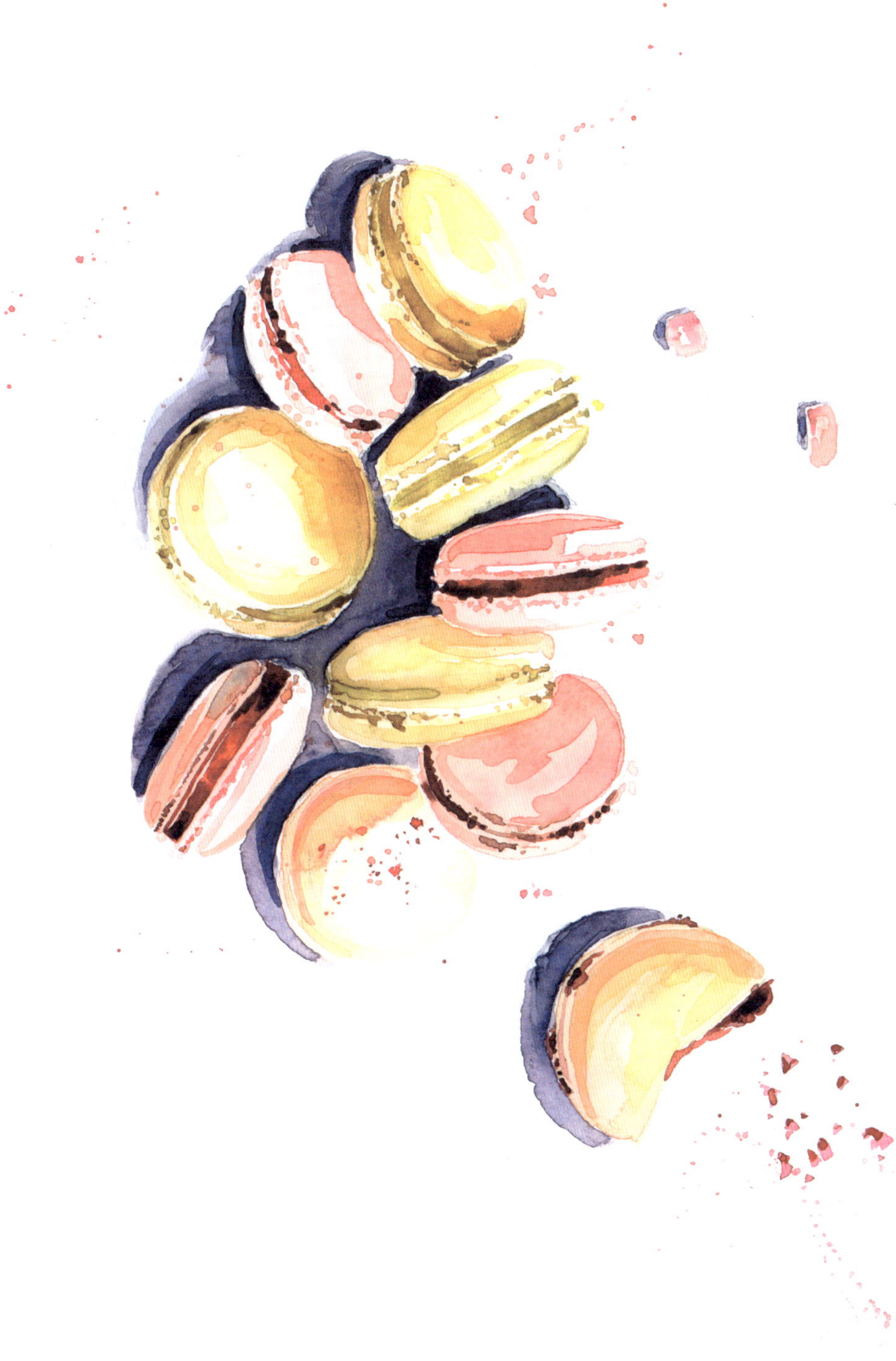

BROWNIES

Step by Step

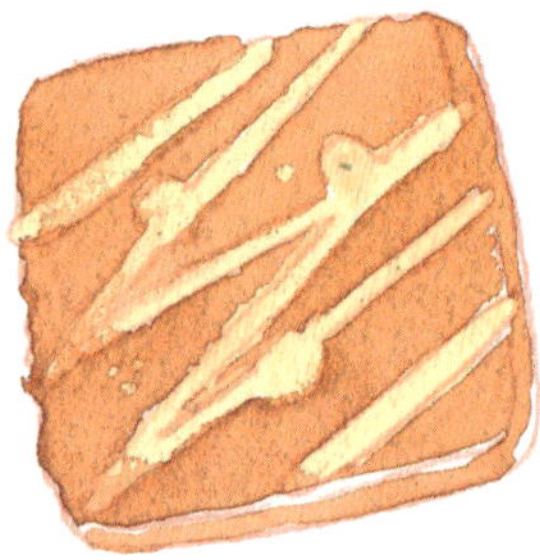

1 Draw the brownies and leave blank spaces for the caramel sauce and hazelnut chunks using masking fluid (shown in light yellow here). Working wet-on-wet, lay down an ochre wash.

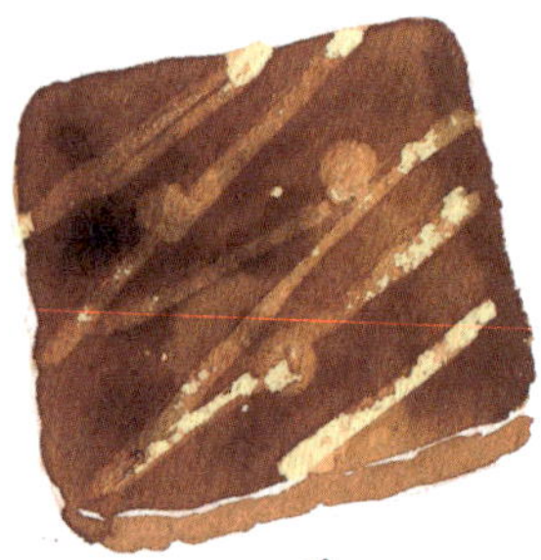

2 Still working wet-on-wet, blend different shades of brown and chocolate. Working dry-on-dry, bring out the shadows.

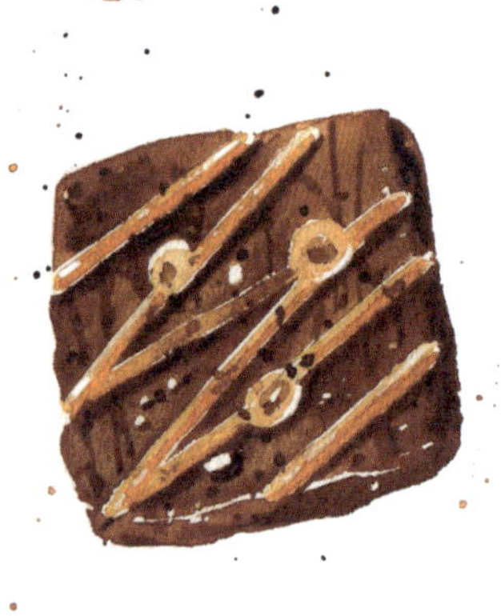

3 Remove the masking fluid with an eraser. Continue highlighting the shadows. Paint the caramel sauce with shades of yellow and orange. To finish off, gently splatter brown paint around the brownies.

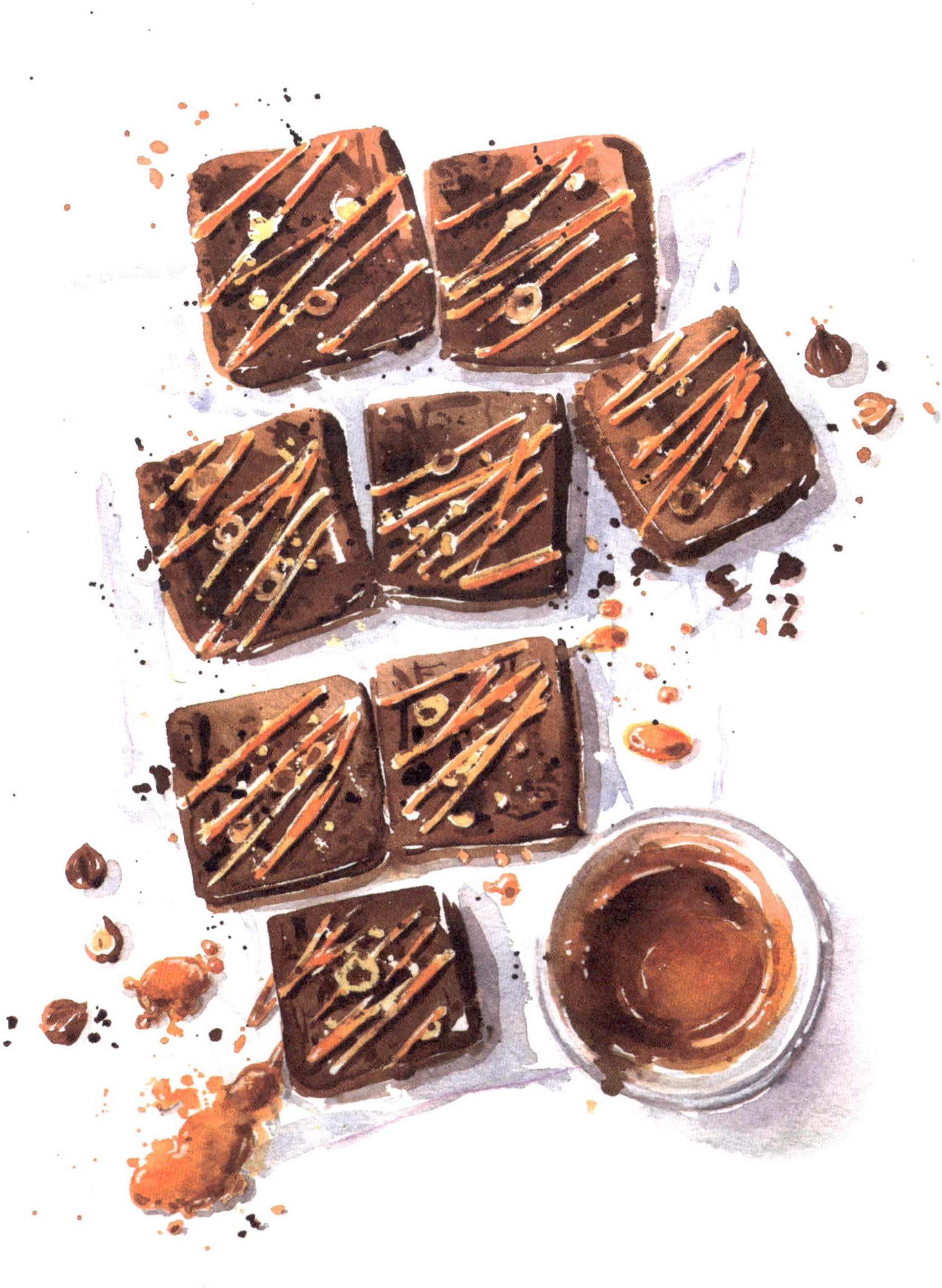

SPRING FLAVORS

Inspiration

SPRING IS FINALLY HERE—A PURE EXPLOSION OF COLOR! IT'S TIME TO CELEBRATE, PLANT, GROW, AND LOVE!

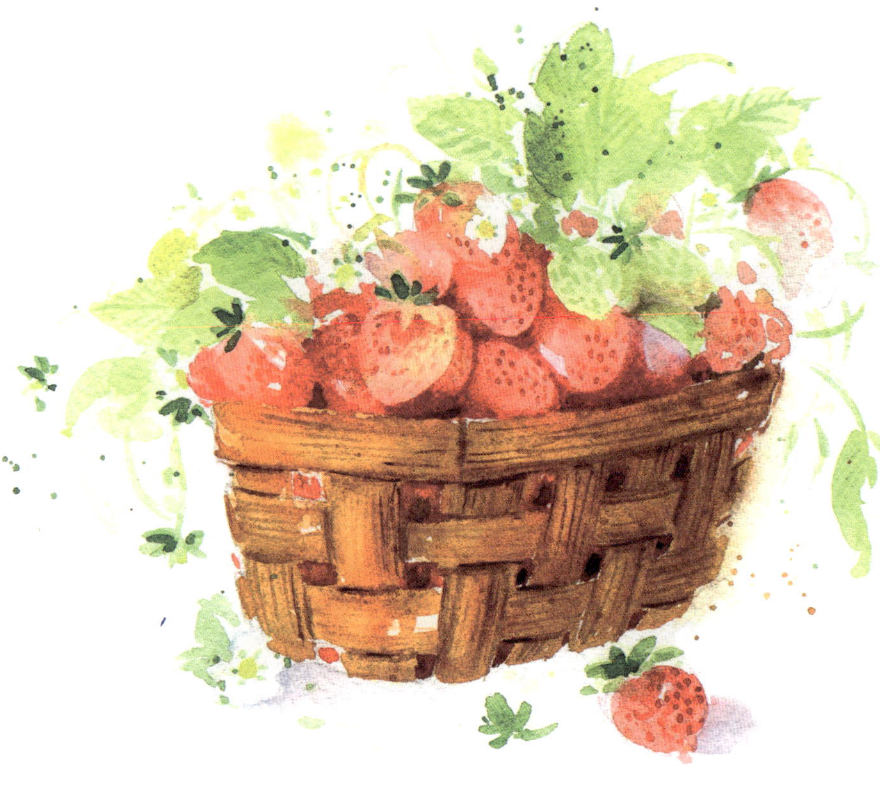

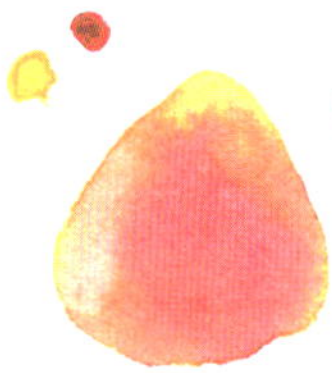

Blend yellow and quinacridone rose on the paper, then make the whole berry darker with a hint of wisteria and permanent red.

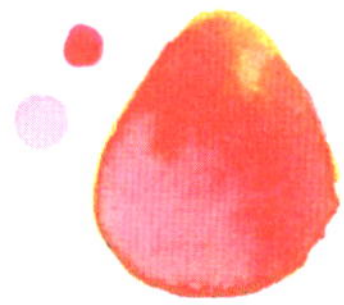

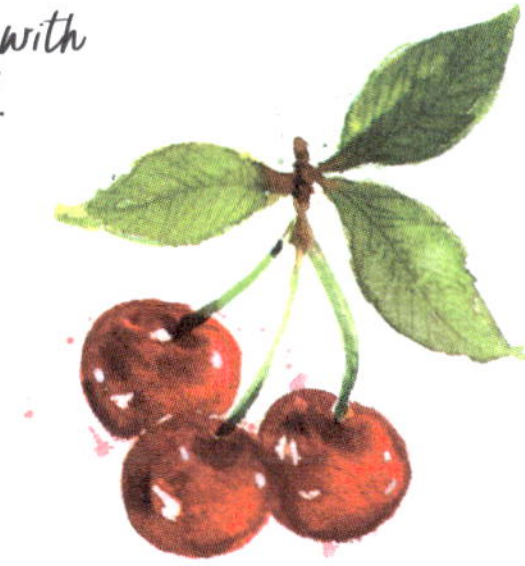

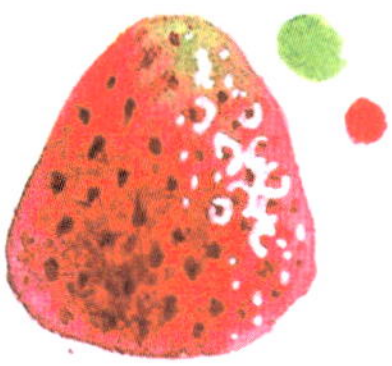

On the first layer of quinacridone purple blue, blend in splotches of cobalt blue and quinacridone rose.

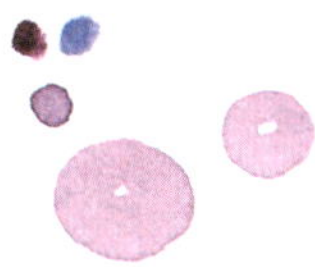

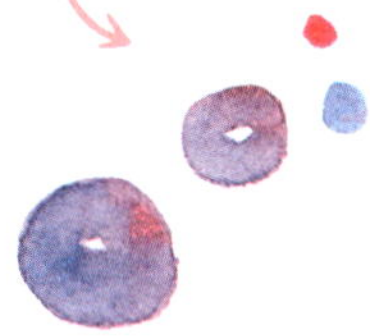

Add diluted sap green and a darker mixture of permanent red as shown, and don't forget to add the strawberry seeds, working dry-on-dry!

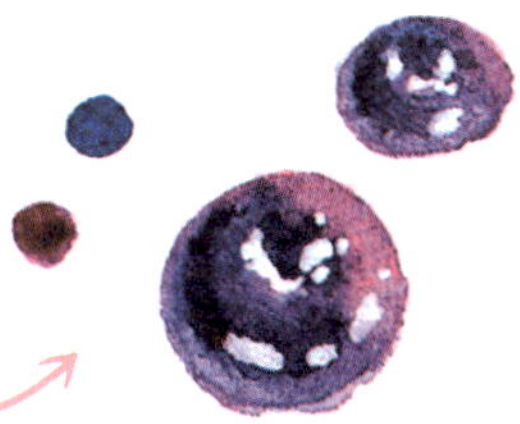

Make the whole berry darker using ultramarine deep and quinacridone purple blue, and finish it off with highlights using a white gel pen. If you want to add more detail, paint stems and leaves on the berries as shown.

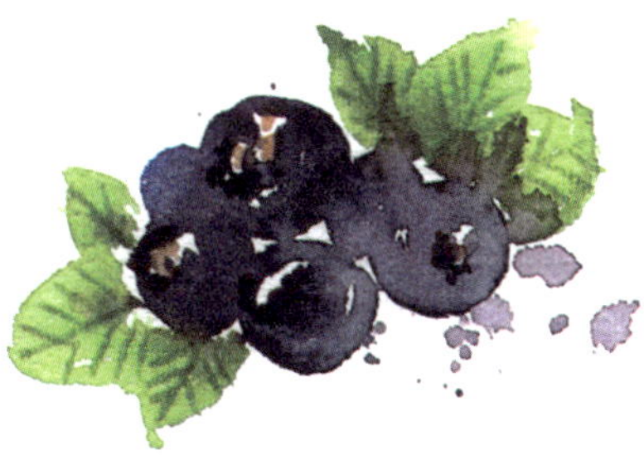

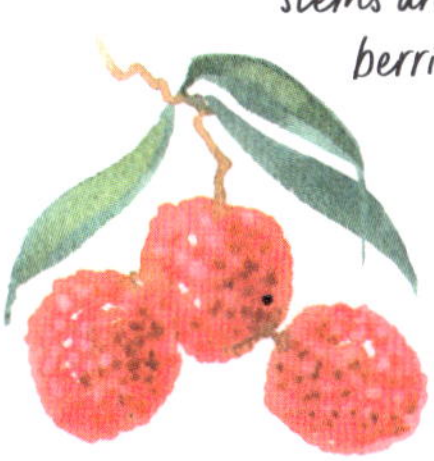

BLUEBERRY CAKE

Inspiration

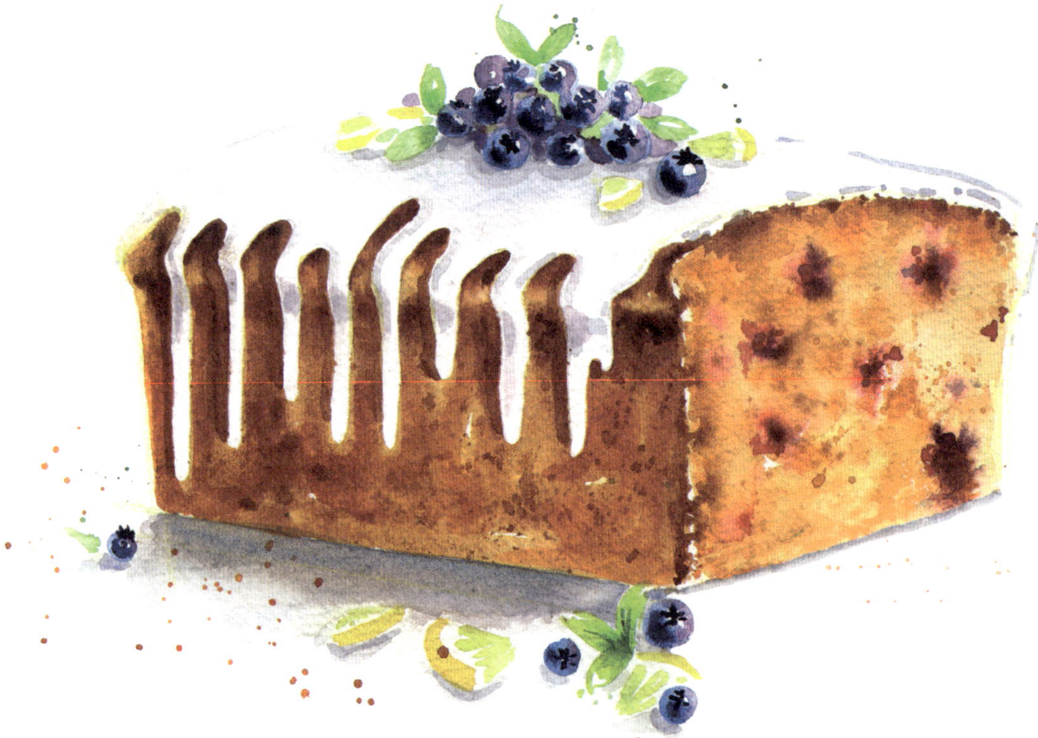

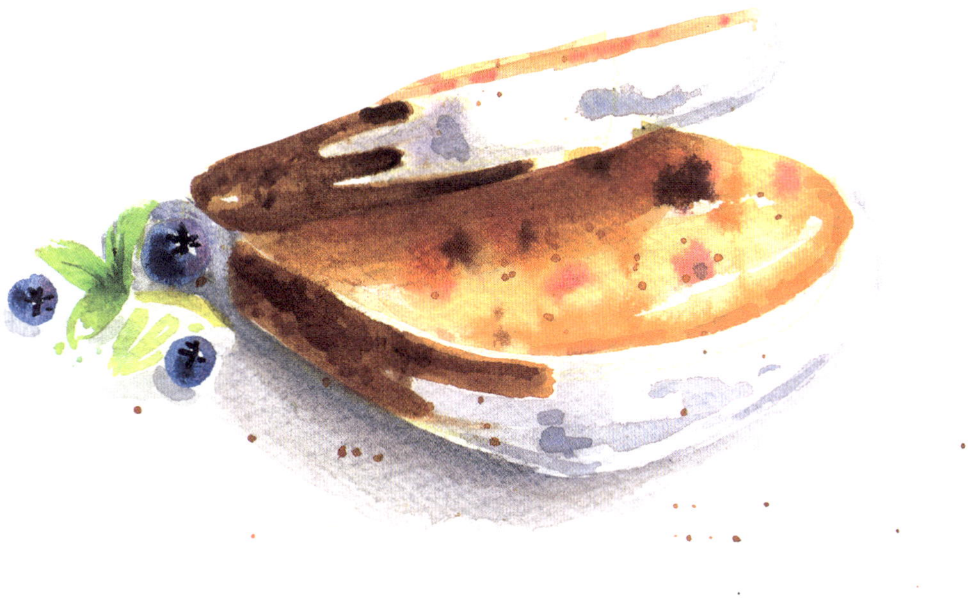

ORANGE CAKE

Recipe

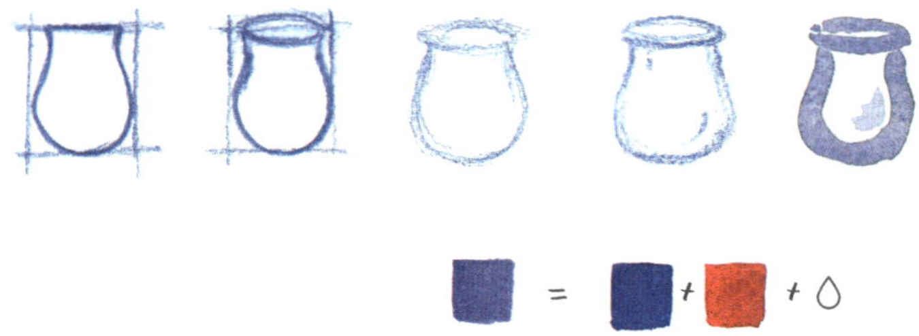

You need at least three values of one color to create volume and contrast.

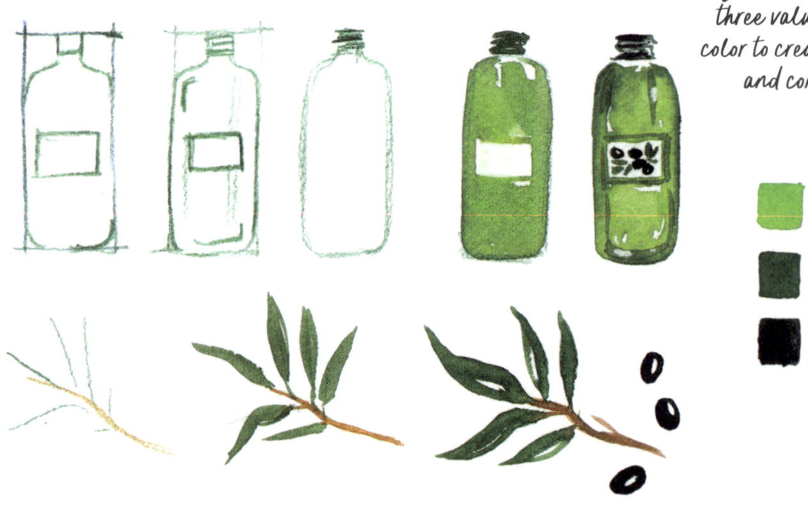

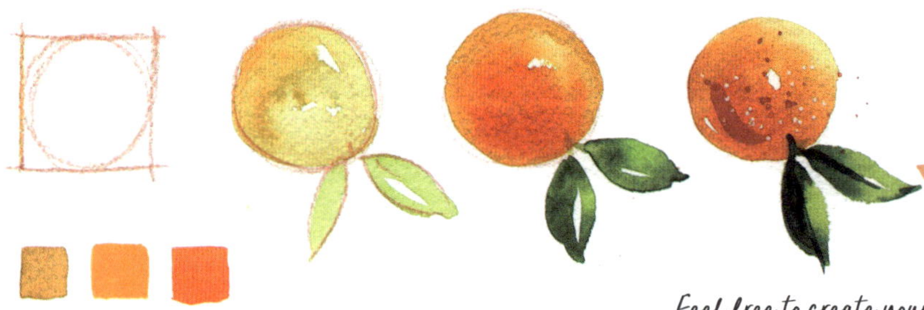

Feel free to create your own mixtures to better render the texture and color of oranges.

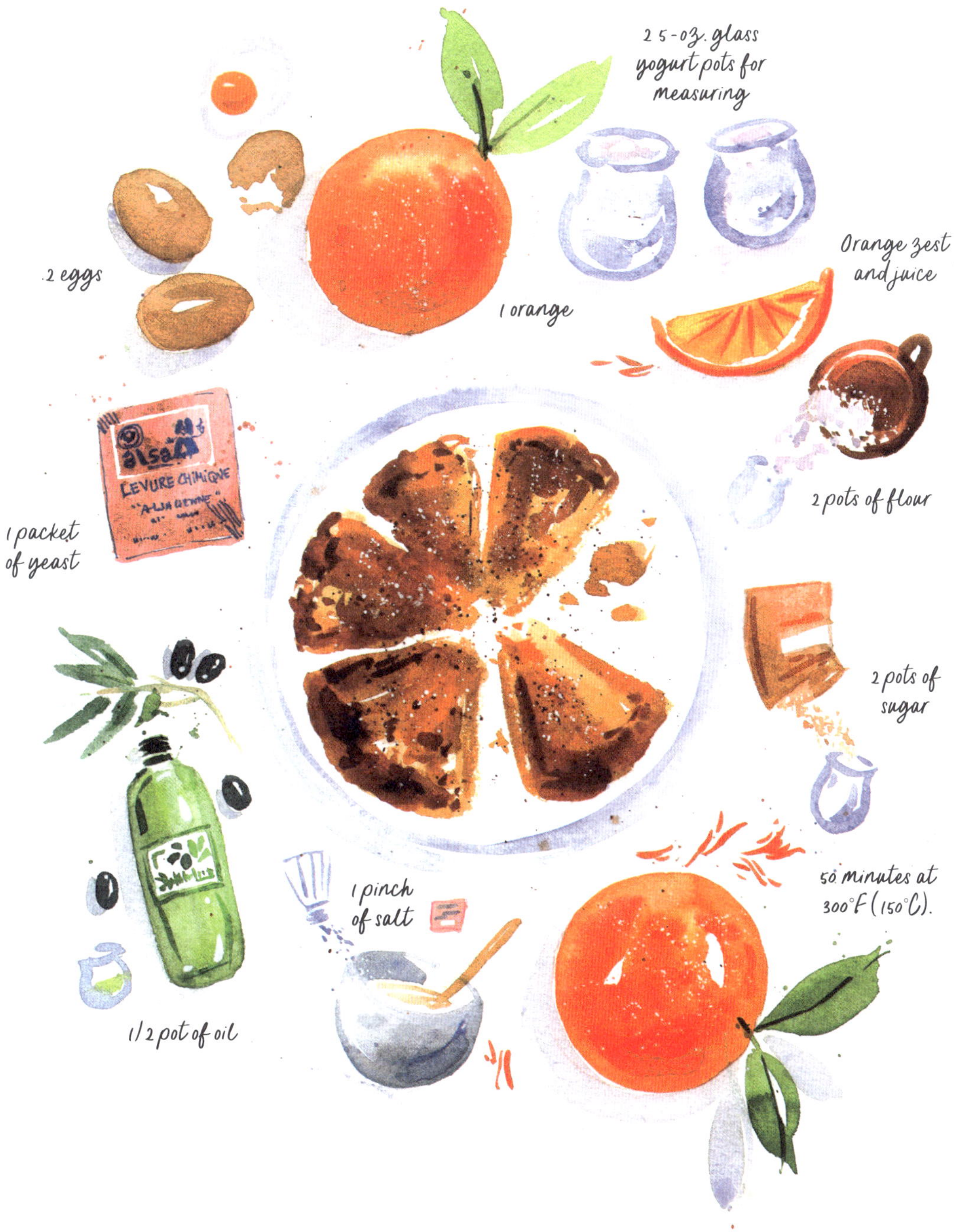
2 5-oz. glass yogurt pots for measuring
2 eggs
1 orange
Orange zest and juice
1 packet of yeast
2 pots of flour
2 pots of sugar
1 pinch of salt
50 minutes at 300°F (150°C).
1/2 pot of oil
alsa
LEVURE CHIMIQUE

DONUTS

Step by Step

I LOVE THE BRIGHT COLORS OF DONUTS, AND PINK ONES ARE MY DAUGHTERS' FAVORITE.

1 Sketch a donut and, working wet-on-wet and using a cat's-tongue or Filbert brush, lay down a pink-powdered-sugar wash. Lift off paint from areas where the light reflects.

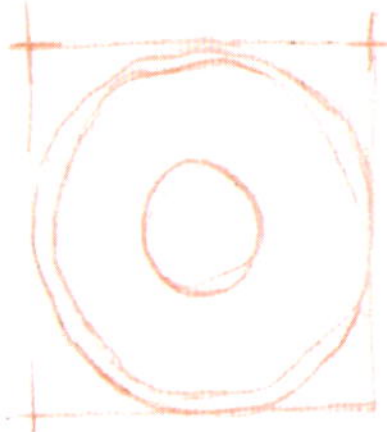

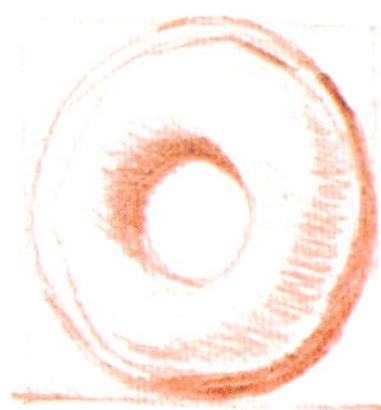

2 Working wet-on-wet, bring out the shadows in the icing with a bolder pink. Lay down a light-ochre wash onto the dough ring, while leaving a narrow gap between the paints to prevent the colors from running into one another.

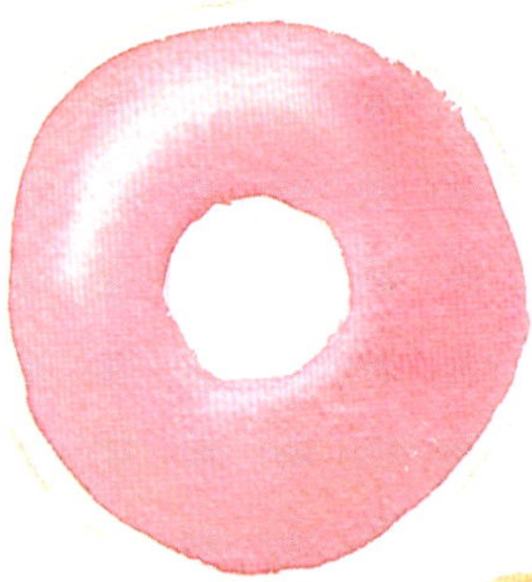

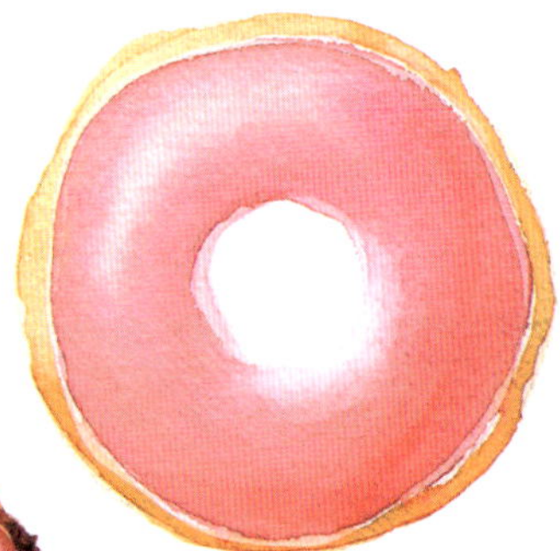

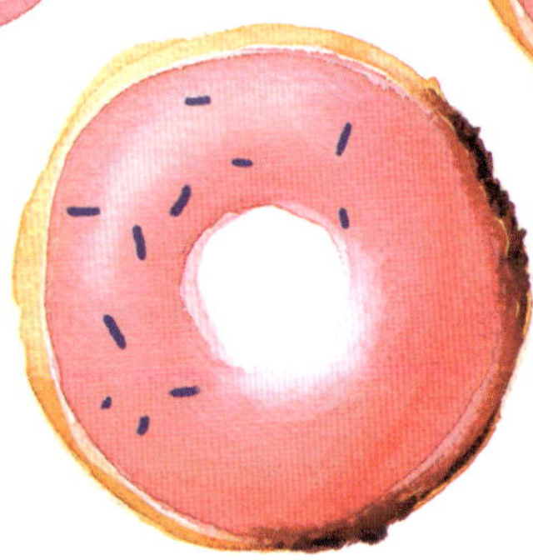

3 Bring out the shadows. Working dry-on-dry, draw sprinkles with paint markers. To finish it off, paint the shadows with a diluted mauve-gray mixture and add light reflections with a white paint marker.

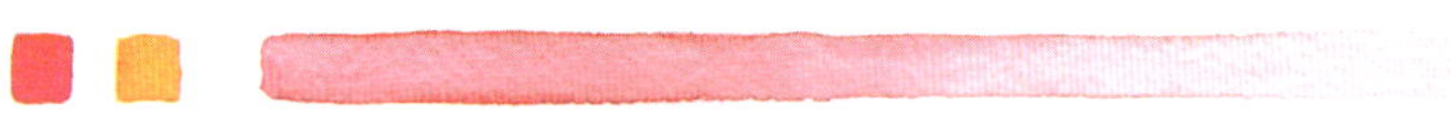

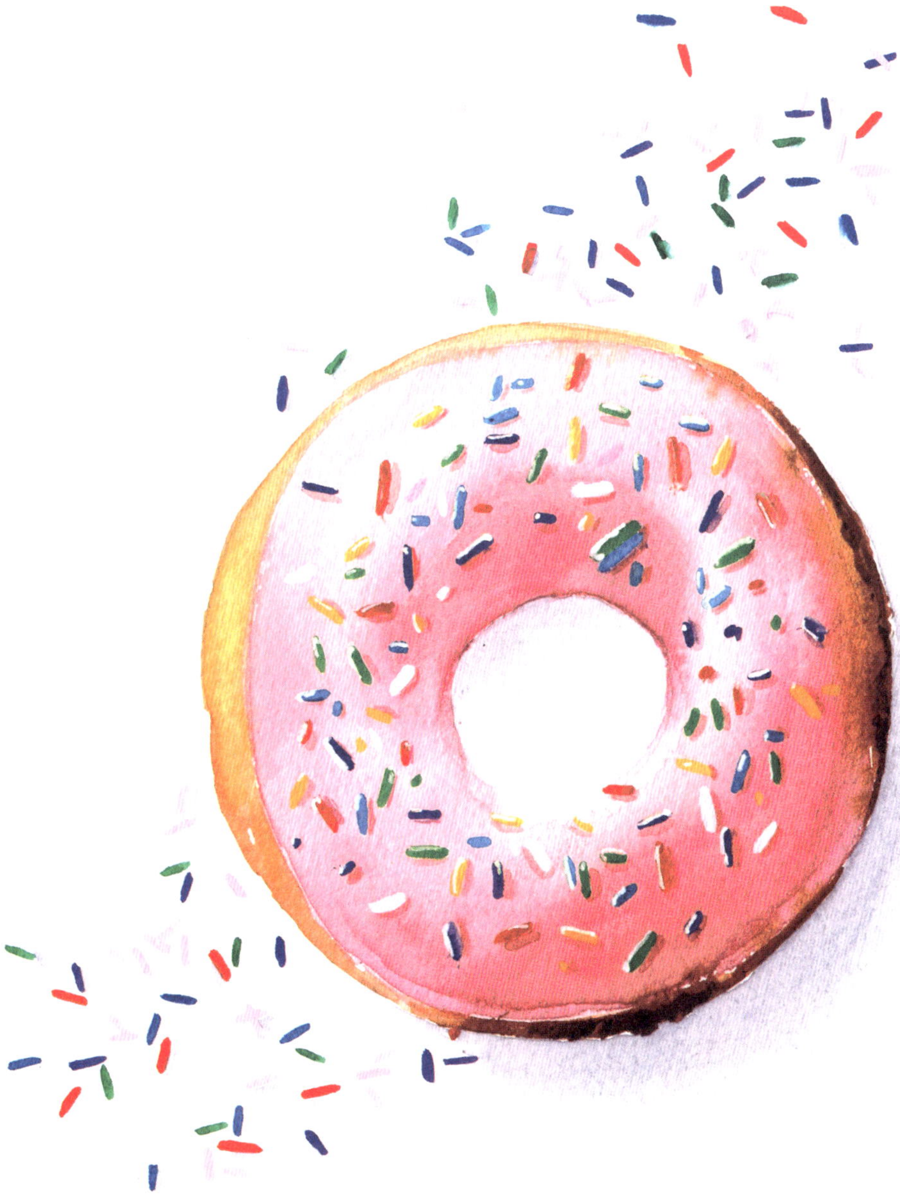

LOLLIPOPS

Step by Step

LOLLIPOPS ALWAYS MAKE ME THINK OF THAT SONG BY THE ARCHIES WHERE THEY SING, "SUGAR, OH, HONEY, HONEY. YOU ARE MY CANDY GIRL!"—IT EVEN MAKES MY PAINTBRUSH BOOGIE!

1 Sketch the lollipop with an erasable pencil and lay down a bright, light-pink wash. Leave blank spaces for the light reflections.

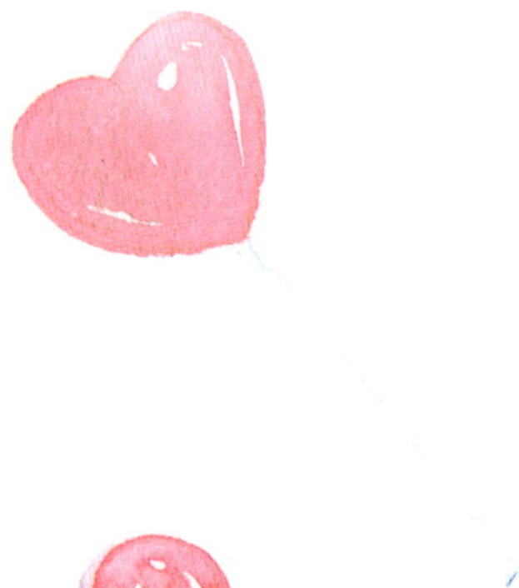

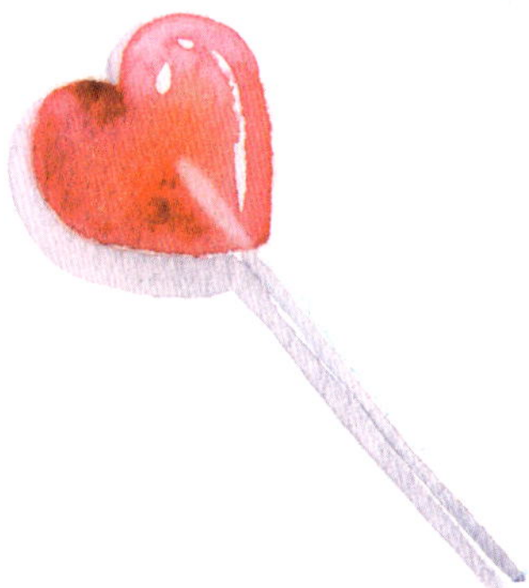

2 Working wet-on-wet, lay down an orange-pink wash, then add bold pink on the left and blend the two. Be careful to avoid the blank space of the light reflections on the right. To create the stick inside the lollipop, paint a line on the lollipop using the lifting-off technique. Working dry-on-dry, paint the drop shadow next to the lollipop.

3 Bring out the shadows on the top of the heart and the left side of the stick by using a more pigmented paint mix. Working dry-on-dry, accentuate the shadow by adding a fine mauve-gray line along the edge of the lollipop.

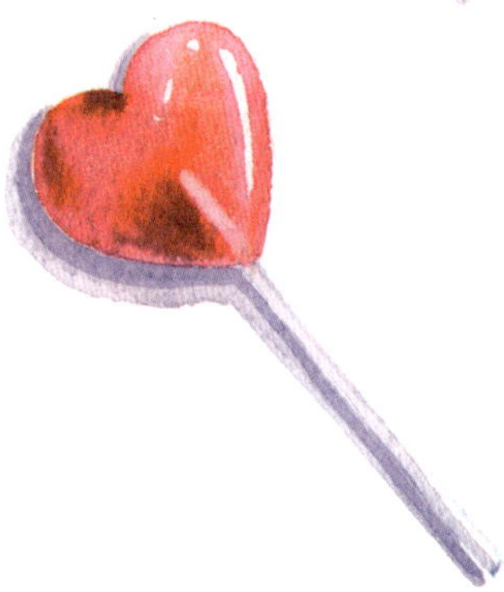

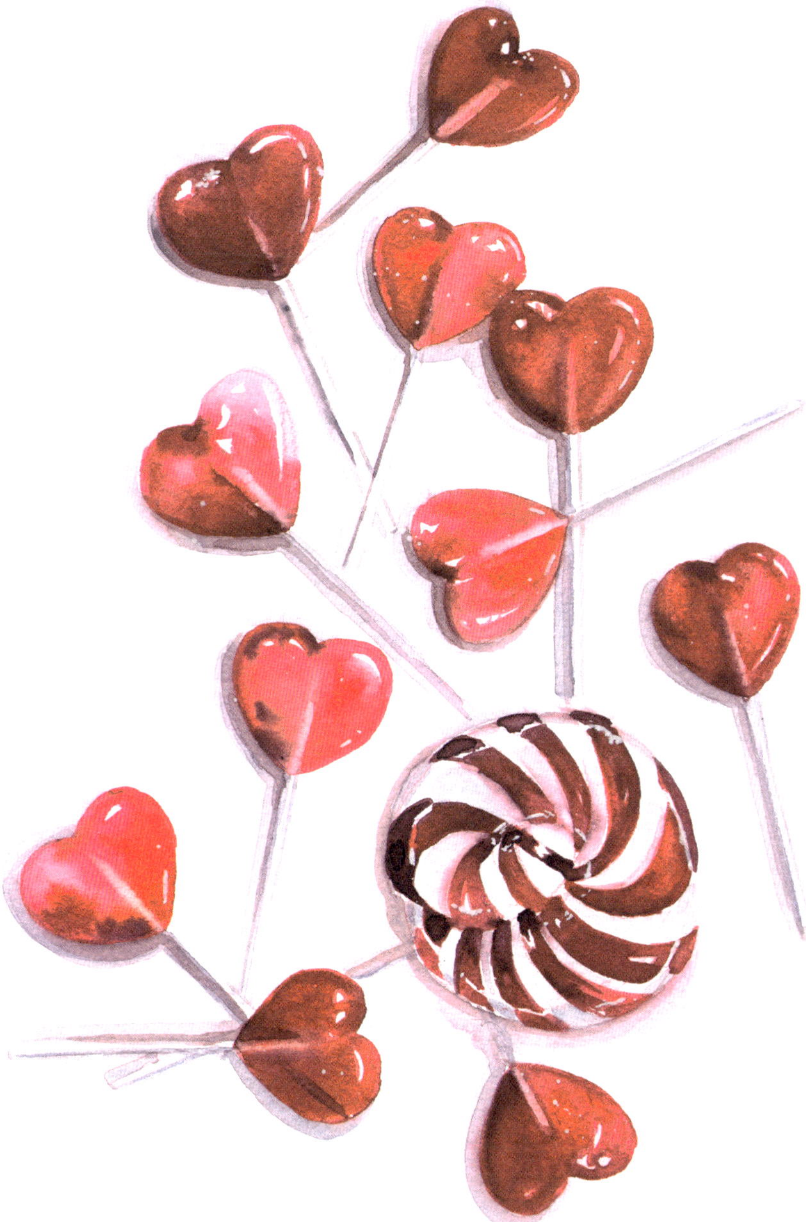

CUPCAKES

Recipe

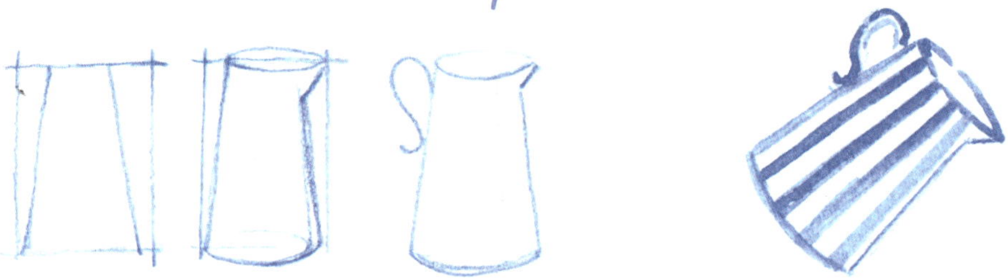

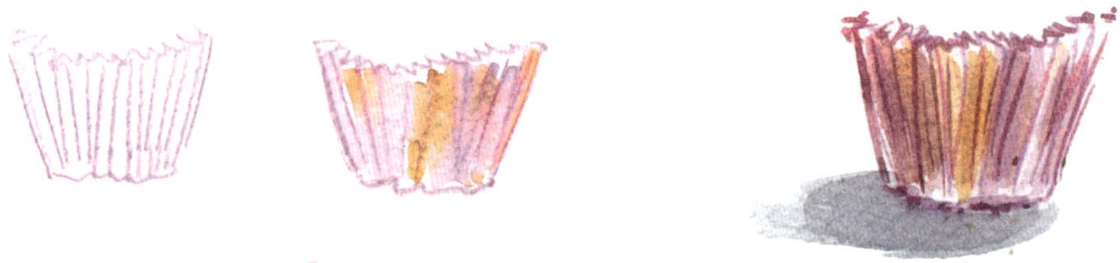

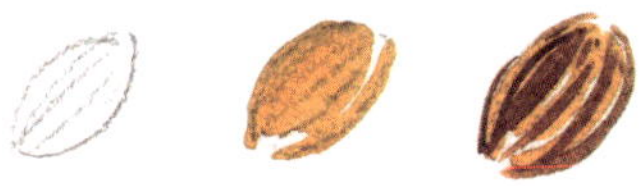

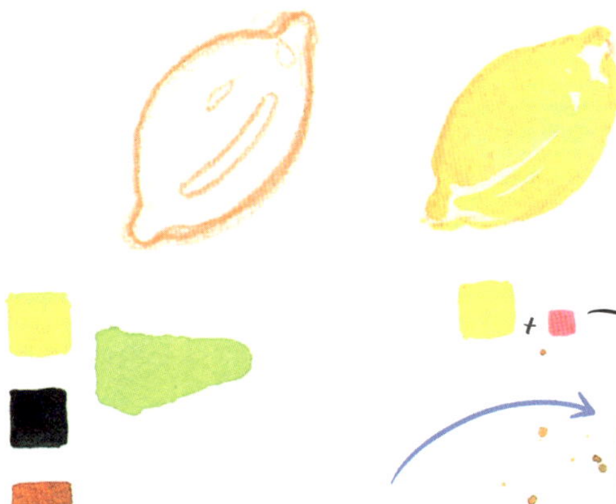

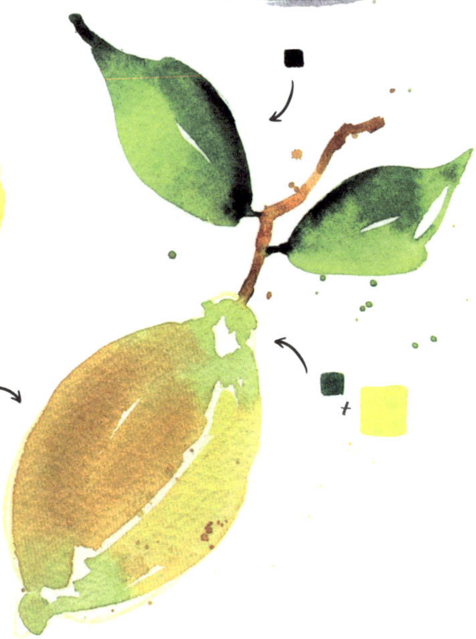

For the lemon, I used lemon yellow, sap green, and opera pink. The yellow and green blend to create a moss green.

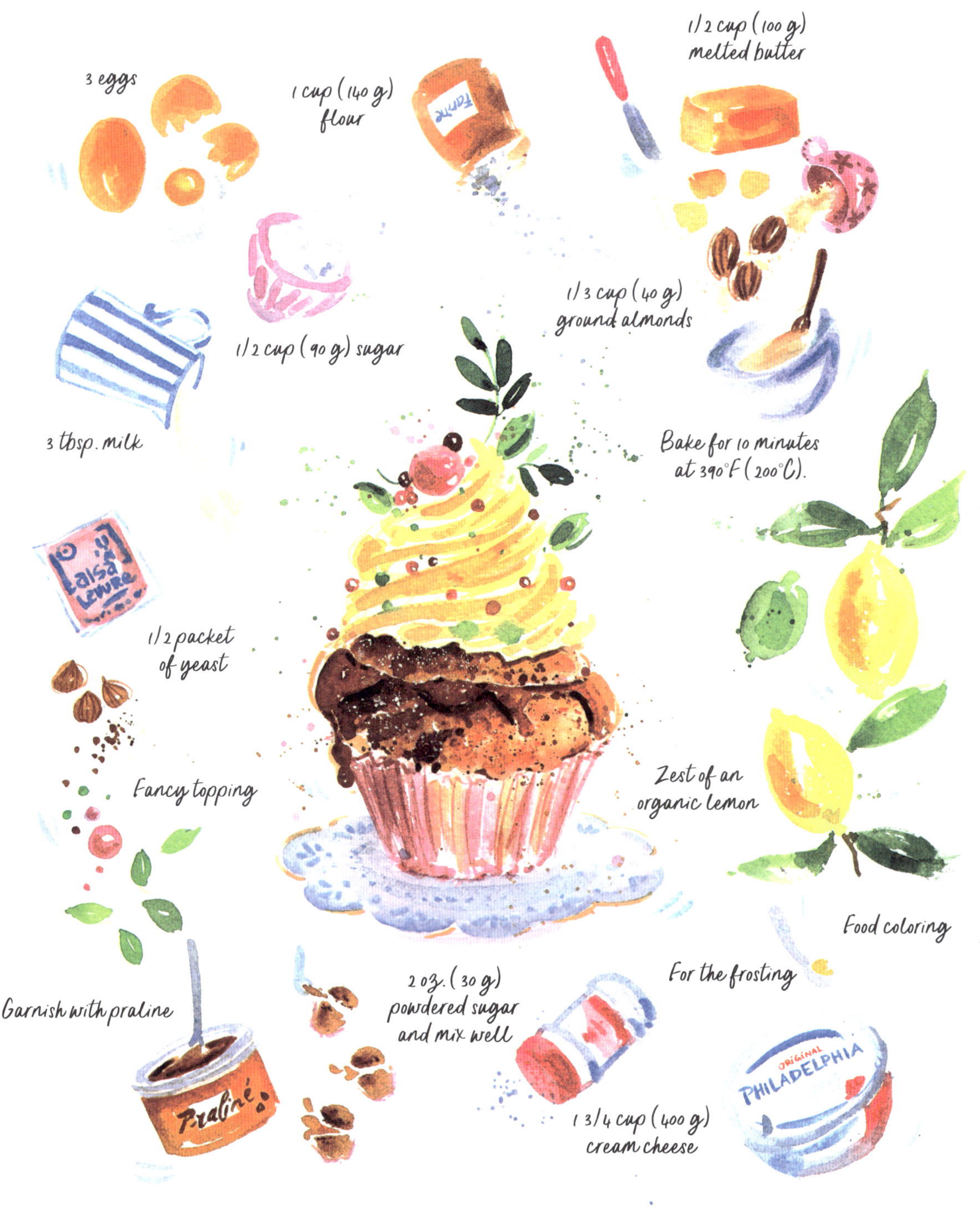
3 eggs
1 cup (140 g) flour
farine
1/2 cup (100 g) melted butter
1/2 cup (90 g) sugar
1/3 cup (40 g) ground almonds
3 tbsp. milk
Bake for 10 minutes at 390°F (200°C).
alsa levure
1/2 packet of yeast
Fancy topping
Zest of an organic lemon
Food coloring
For the frosting
Garnish with praline
2 oz. (30 g) powdered sugar and mix well
Praliné
ORIGINAL PHILADELPHIA
1 3/4 cup (400 g) cream cheese

MINI TARTS

Step by Step

A COUPLE OF LITTLE PANSIES AS A GARNISH WILL BRING LAST-MINUTE SUNSHINE TO YOUR SPRING DISHES!

1 Sketch a pansy and lay down a pinkish-mauve-gray wash where the bottom petals will go. Lay down a light-blue wash where the upper ones will be. Make sure to reserve blank spaces by leaving the paper white in a few spots.

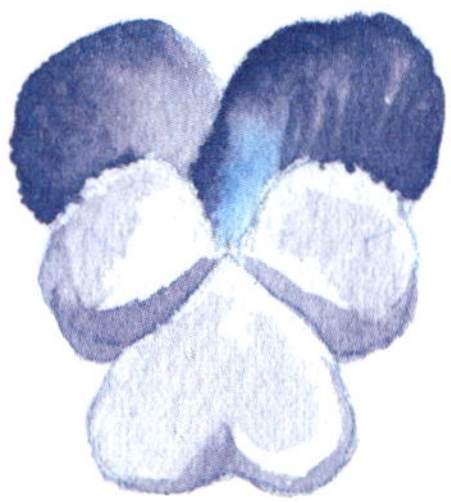

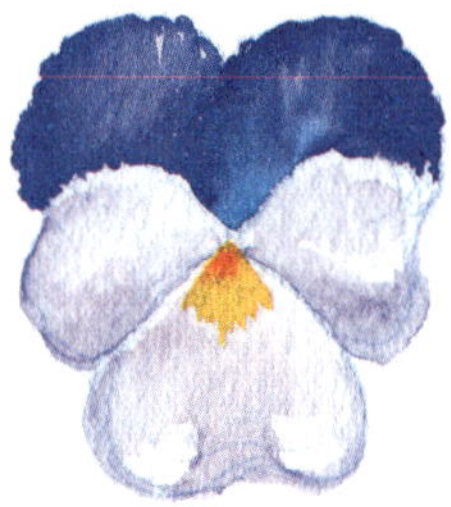

2 Working wet-on-wet, blend the pigments, being careful not to mix the colors for the top petals with the colors for the bottom petals. Working dry-on-dry, paint the pansy's central corolla in light yellow with a drop of orange at the center.

3 Bring out the shadows with a pink wash for the bottom half and a purple wash for the top. Don't forget to keep it quite transparent by diluting the pigments. Working dry-on-dry, draw grooves with a bold blue on the bottom petals and a bold purple on the top petals.

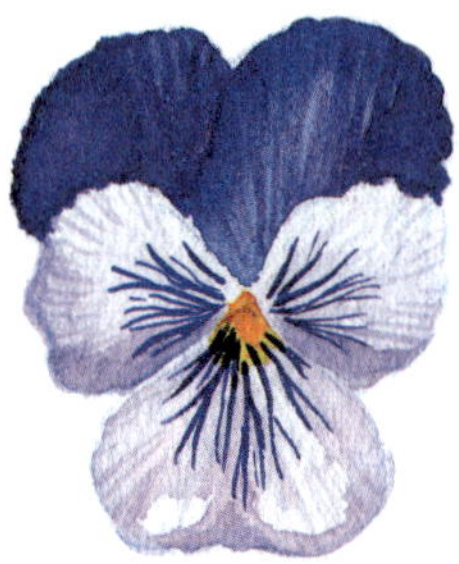

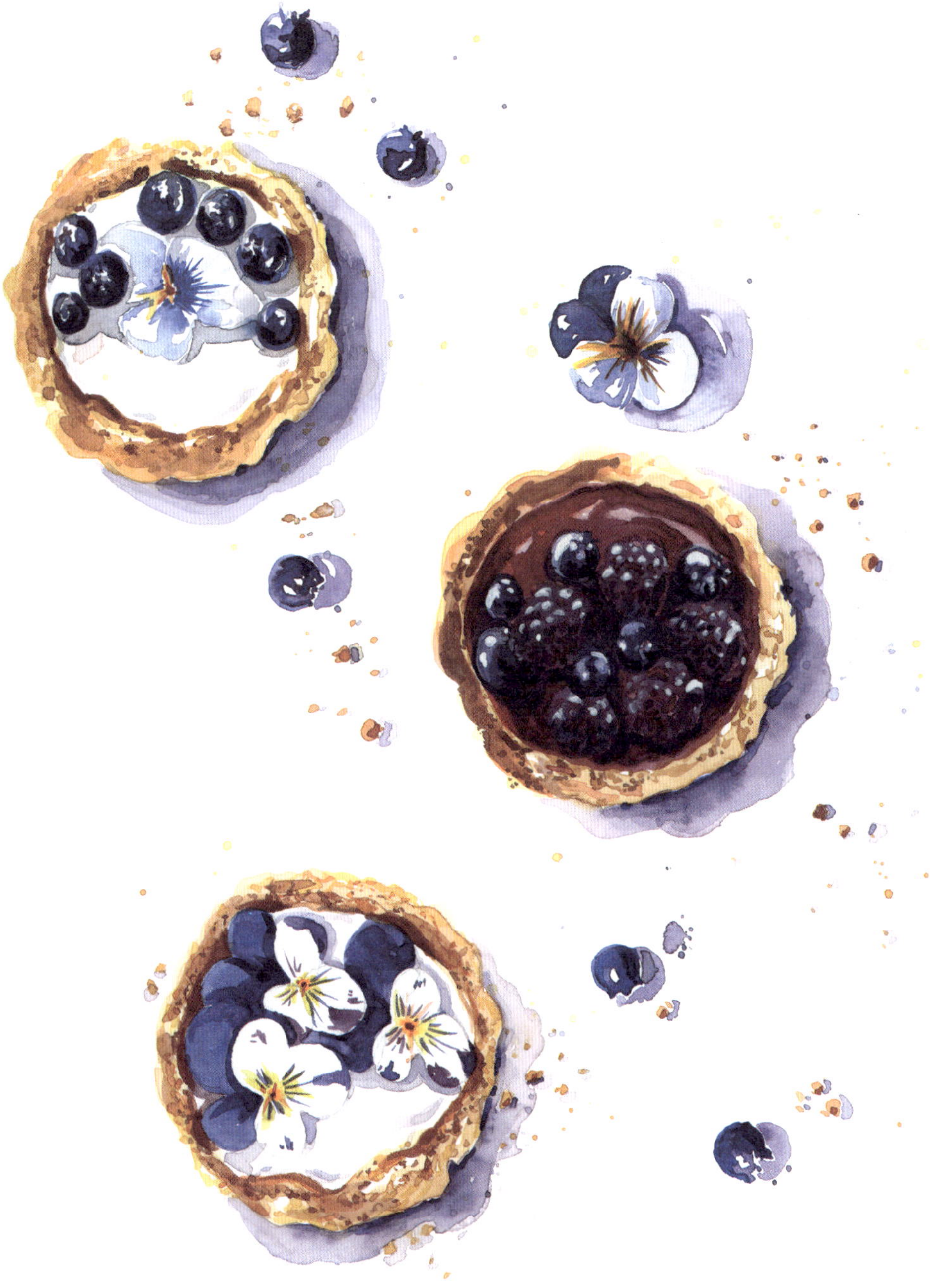

LAYER CAKE

Inspiration

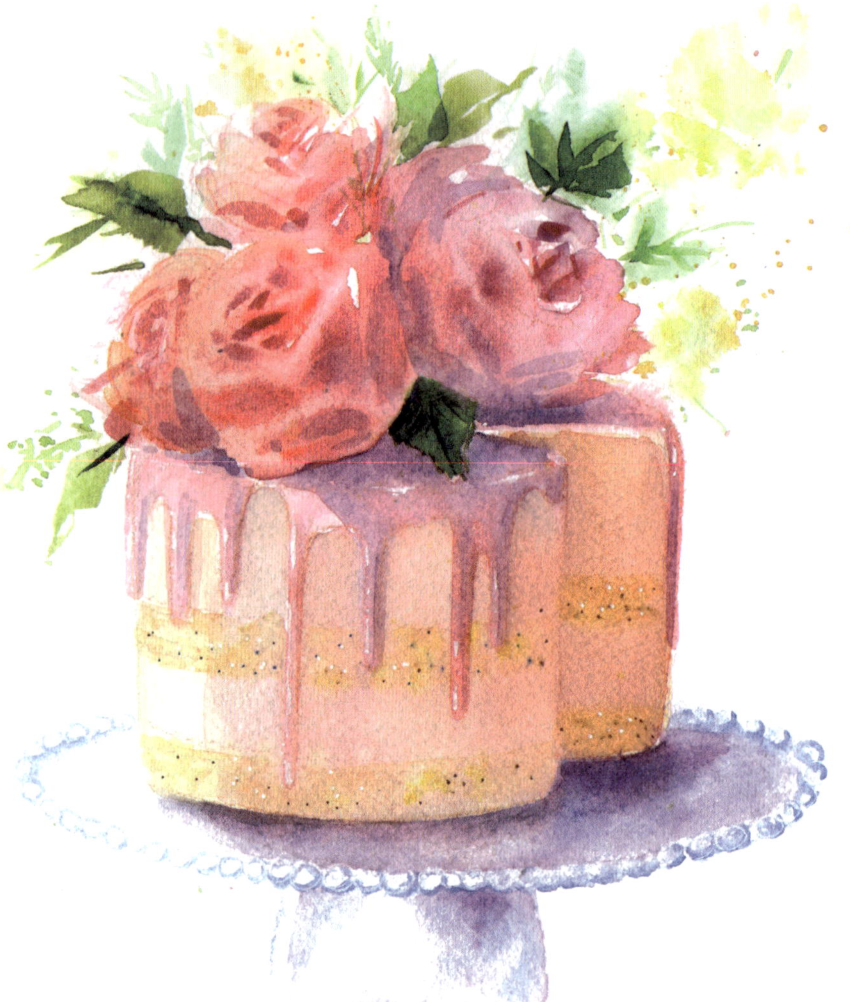

TASTES OF SUMMER

Inspiration

FINALLY, THE LONG SUMMER DAYS ARE HERE, ALONG WITH GOOD TIMES, BRIGHT COLORS, AND WARMTH! SUMMER IN THE SUNSHINE, HOW SWEET THAT SOUNDS!

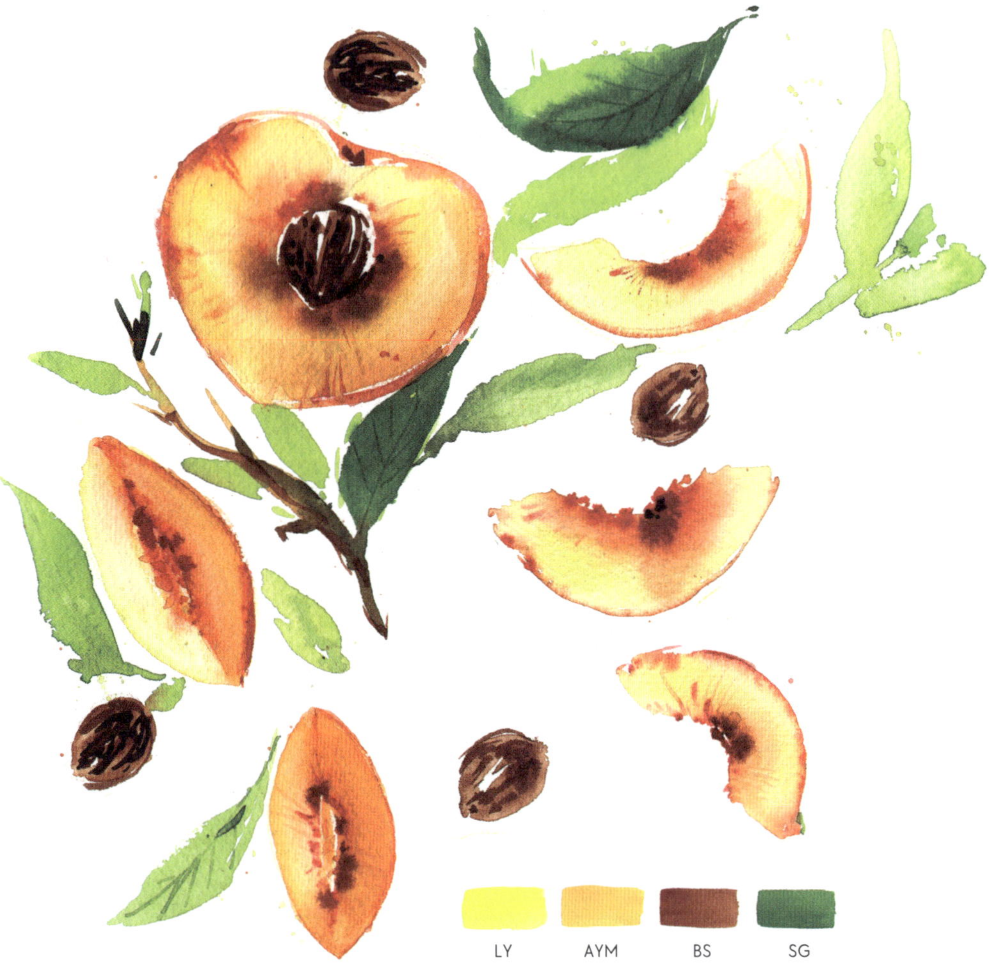

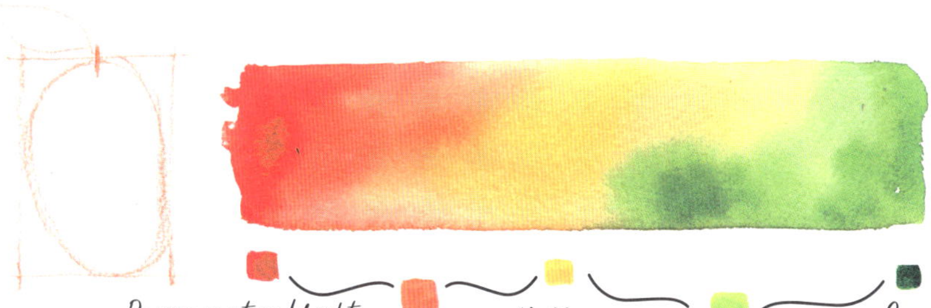

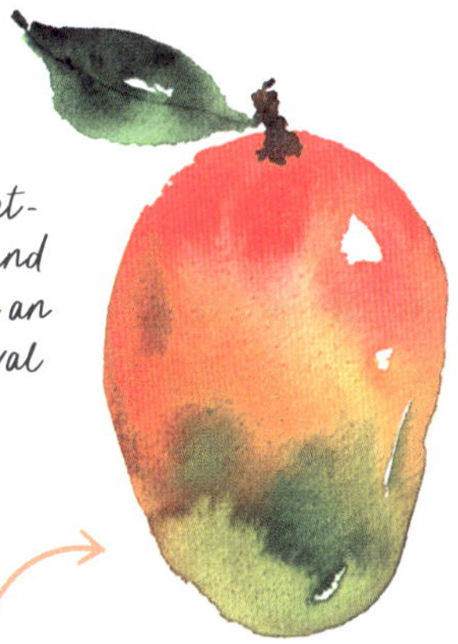

Working wet-on-wet, blend the colors in an irregular oval shape.

Be careful not to mix green and red together, since these two complementary colors can neutralize one another, which diminishes their vibrancy.

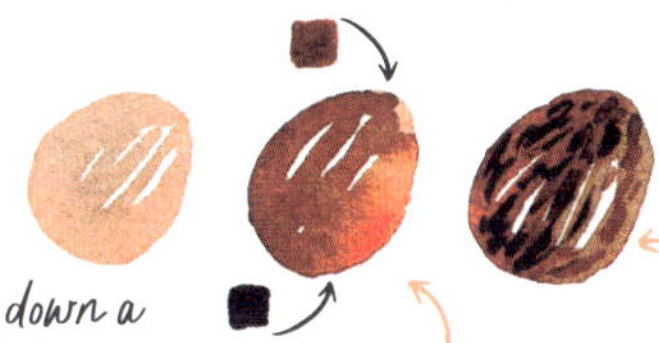

Lay down a light-brown wash.

Working wet-on-wet, bring out the blends by adding burnt sienna and burnt umber.

Think about the direction the light is coming from, and leave blank spaces for reflections.

Working dry-on-dry, streak the pit with a slightly diluted pigment.

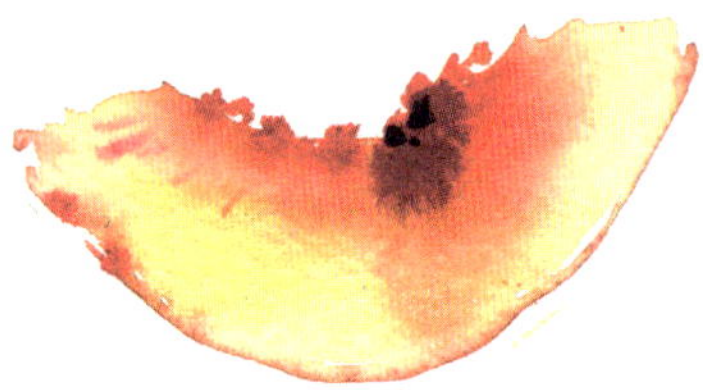

Use madder lake deep for shadows and spots and quinacridone rose for a touch of pink.

On a yellow wash, create blends with permanent red light.

Working dry-on-dry, paint orange spots to re-create the velvety appearance of the peach skin.

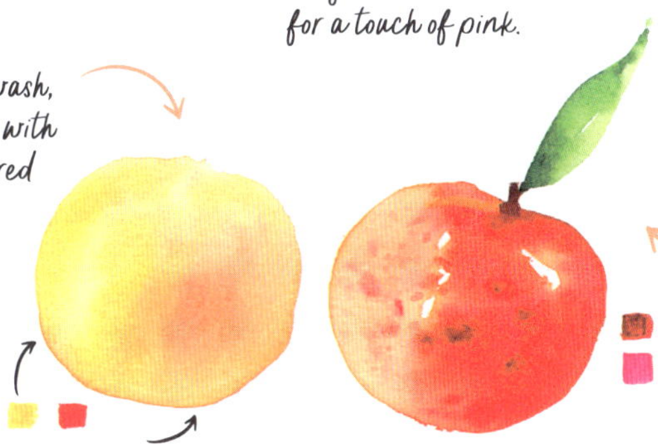

ICE POPS

Step by Step

ICE POPS ARE AN ICONIC SYMBOL OF SUMMER VACATION! YOU CAN PRACTICALLY FEEL THE SUN WARMING YOUR SKIN JUST BY LOOKING AT THEM.

1 Sketch the ice pop. Lay down a very diluted yellow wash where your ice pop and the piece of kiwi will go. Leave thin blank spaces as shown to create the rectangular shapes from the ice-pop mold.

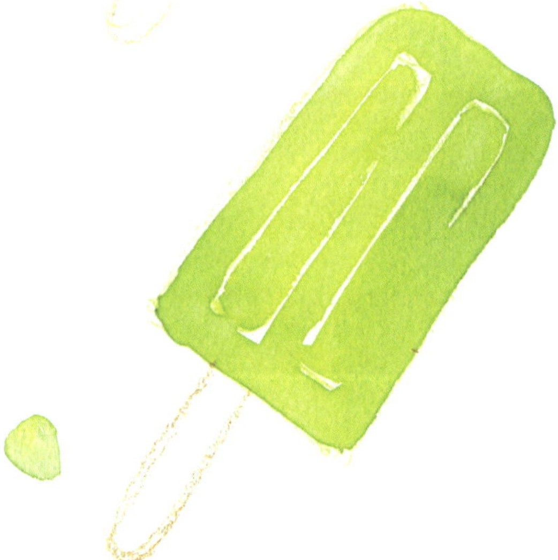

2 Working wet-on-wet, add brushstrokes in a yellowy moss green, taking care not to get paint onto the white spaces that indicate the mold.

3 Using a bolder green, paint thin lines where the shadows on the left-hand side of the ice pop will be, as well as to the left of the rectangular shapes of the mold, always making sure to leave the blank spaces untouched. Lay down an ochre wash for the stick.

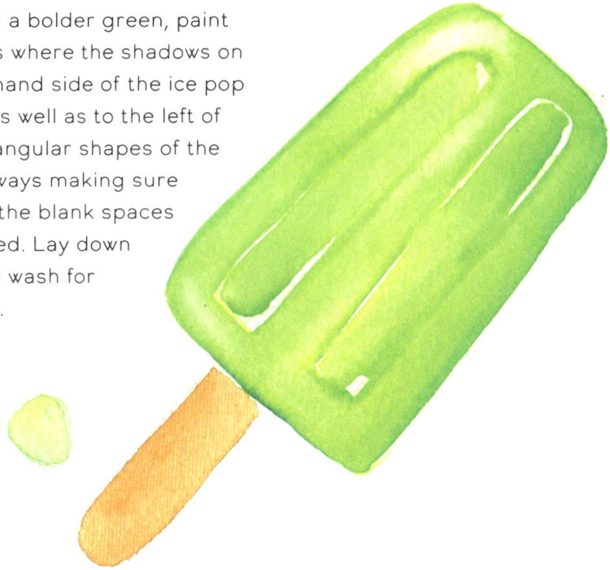

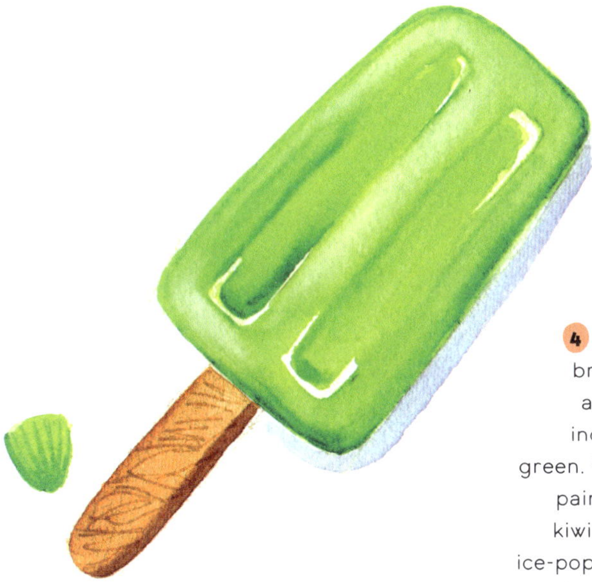

4 Still working wet-on-wet, bring out the shadows with a bolder mixture of green, including a hint of Hooker's green. With this diluted mixture, paint streaks on the piece of kiwi. Draw the streaks on the ice-pop stick with a glass pen or toothpick to create the marbled texture of the wood.

5 Working dry-on-dry, paint the drop shadows. Wet some areas around the ice pop and lay down a yellow-green wash to create the effect of the ice pop melting. Paint the shadow of the stick in a bolder shade of ochre. Make splatters in green and yellow, working both wet-on-wet and dry-on-dry.

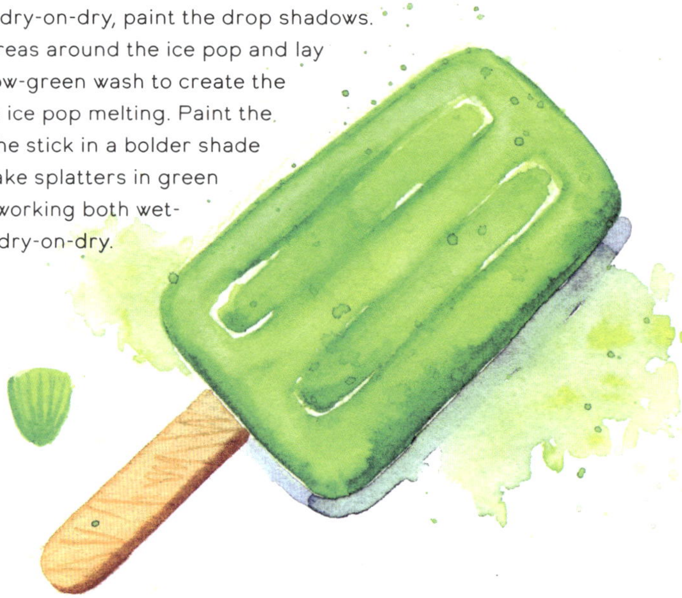

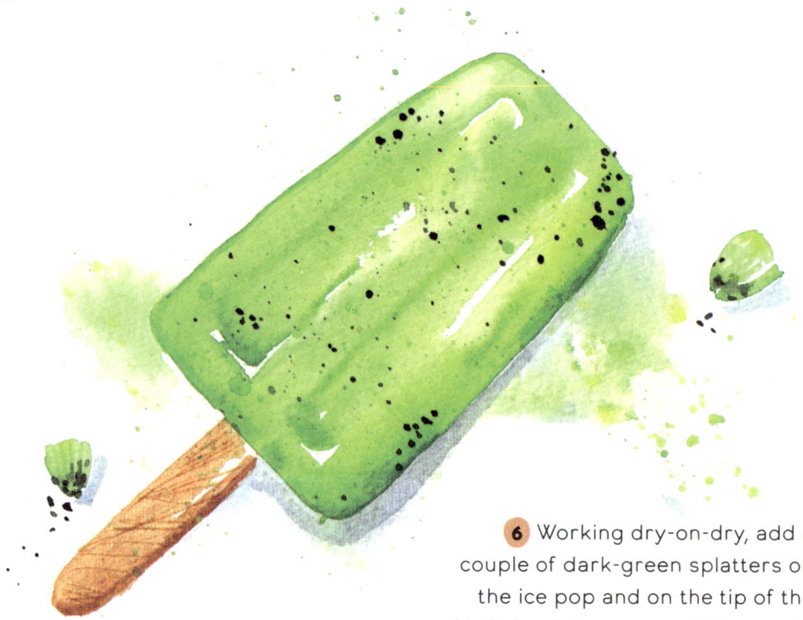

6 Working dry-on-dry, add a couple of dark-green splatters on the ice pop and on the tip of the kiwi chunk to represent the seeds.

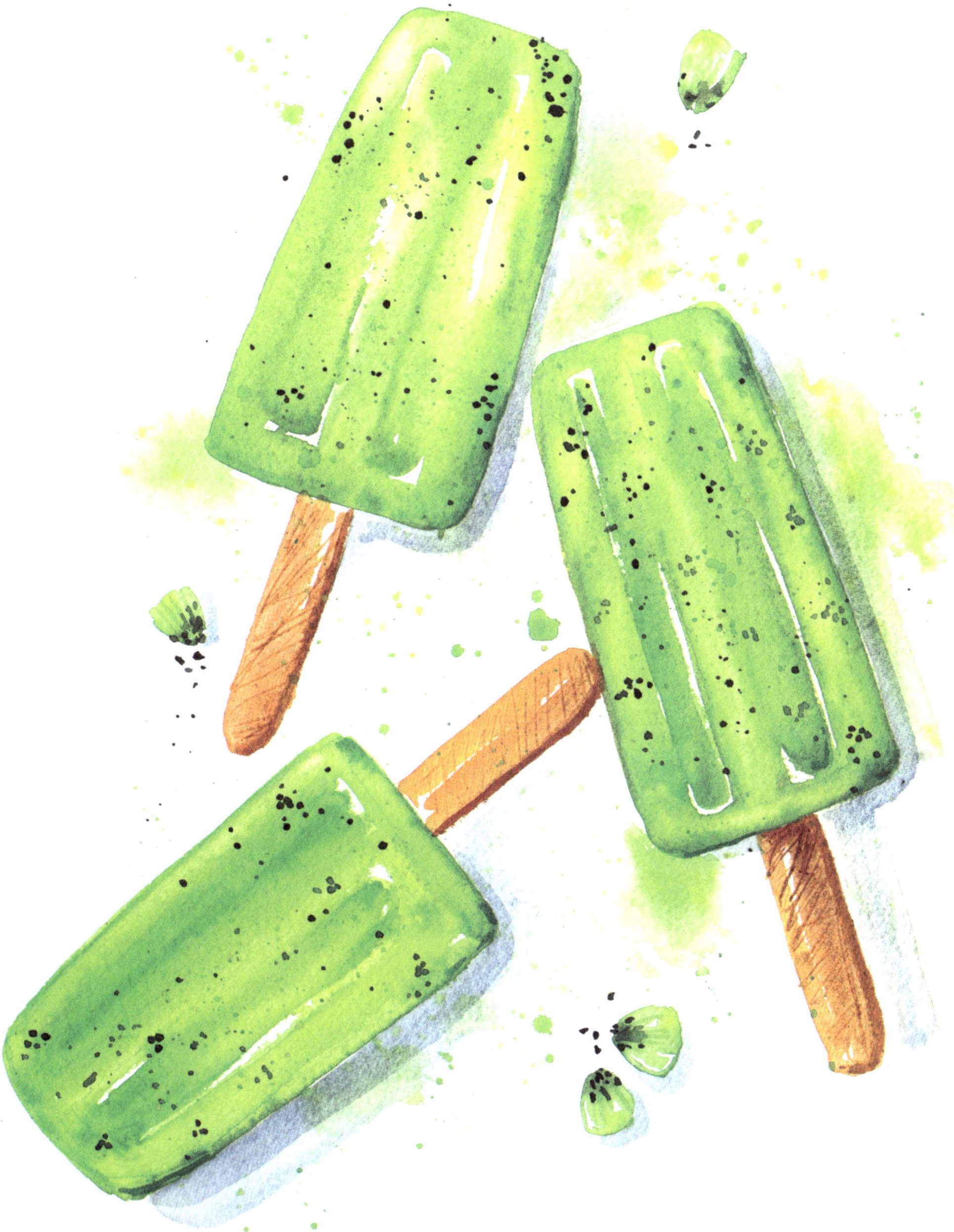

CANDIES GALORE

Step by Step

ON RAINY DAYS, I LOVE LISTENING TO JULIE ANDREWS SINGING "A SPOONFUL OF SUGAR" IN *MARY POPPINS*—THAT'S EXACTLY MY PERSONAL PHILOSOPHY!

1 Lay down a bright-blue wash (cerulean blue) in the shape of a little gummy bear by painting six circles and connecting them all in the center as shown.

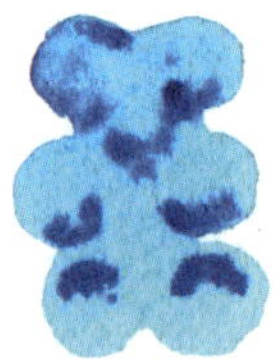

2 Working wet-on-wet, apply pure blue pigment with the tip of your thinnest brush under the ears and on the curves of the paws.

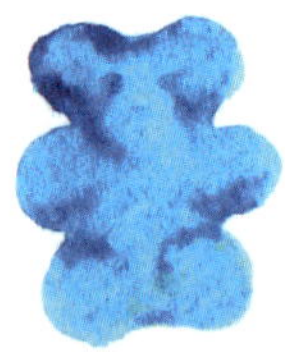

3 Still working wet-on-wet, add more pigment, or remove some if there is too much. Working dry-on-dry, paint two small eyes and a dot for the nose.

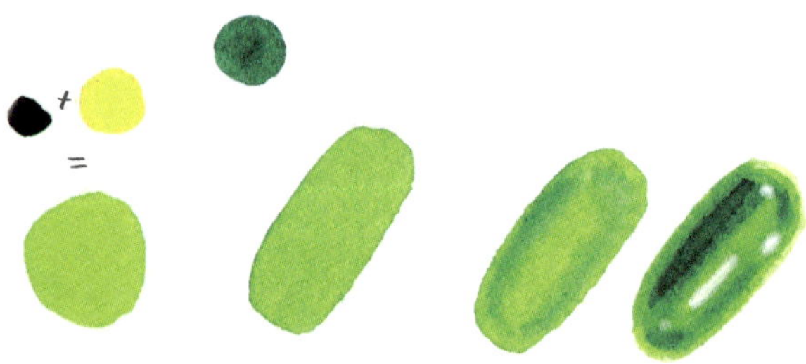

Repeat this method to depict other candies in different shapes and colors.

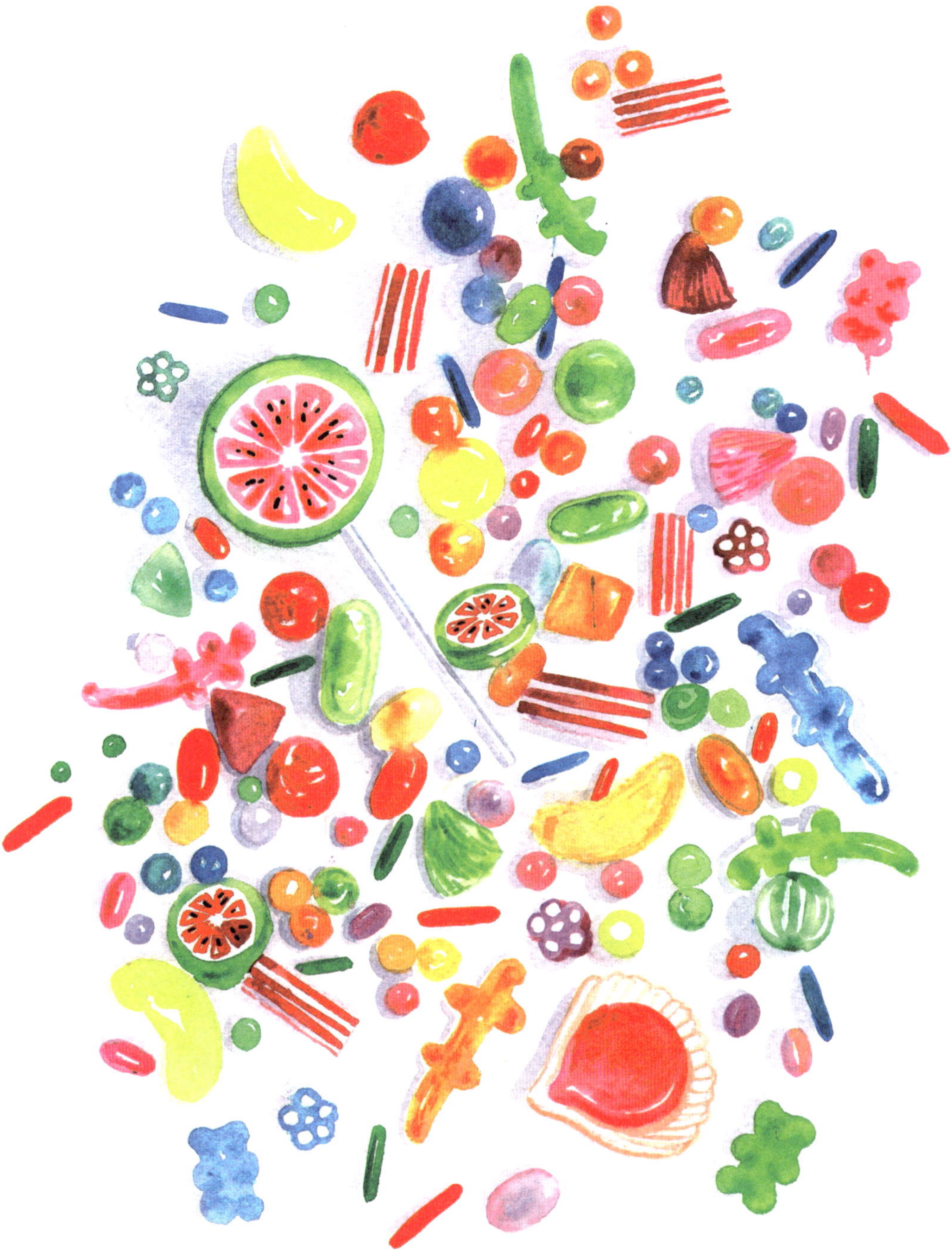

CREAM PUFFS

Inspiration

A monochromatic sketch is very useful for visualizing color values, shadows, and light.

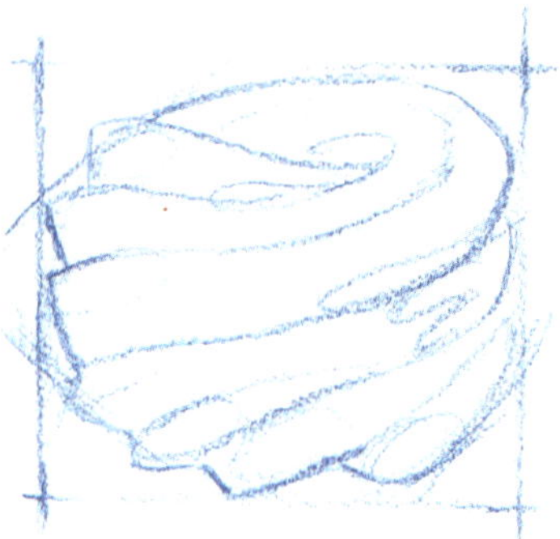

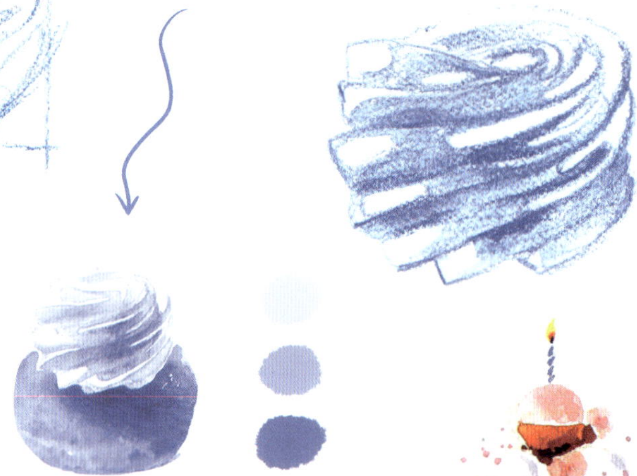

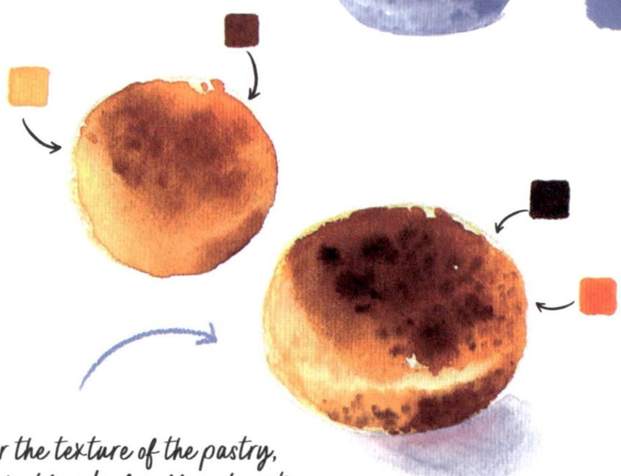

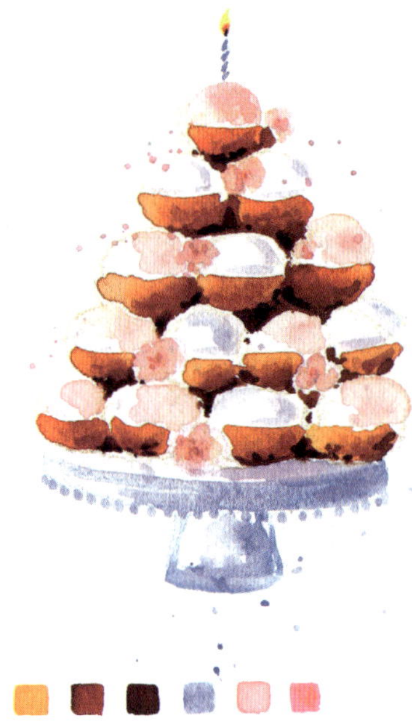

For the texture of the pastry, make blends of yellow, burnt sienna, and burnt umber.

Painting whipped cream is all about your technique for handling color values, volume, and contrasts!

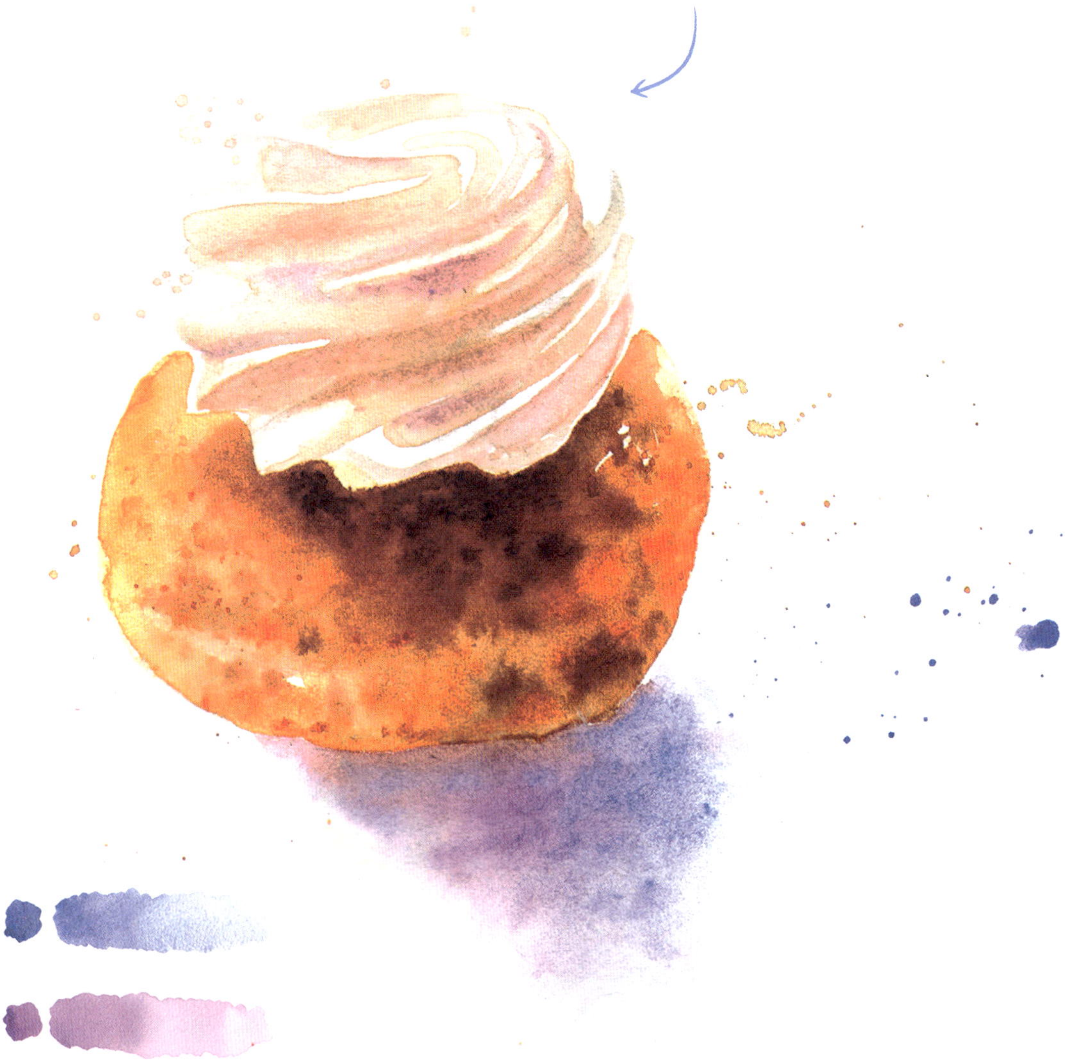

CLAFOUTIS

Recipe

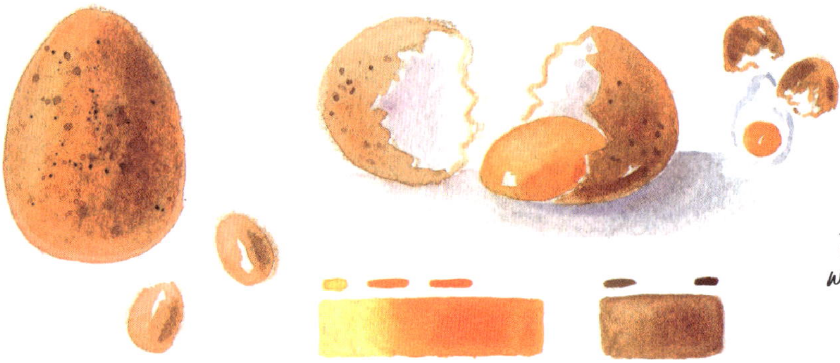

The eggs are painted with a mix of ochre and a drop of sienna.

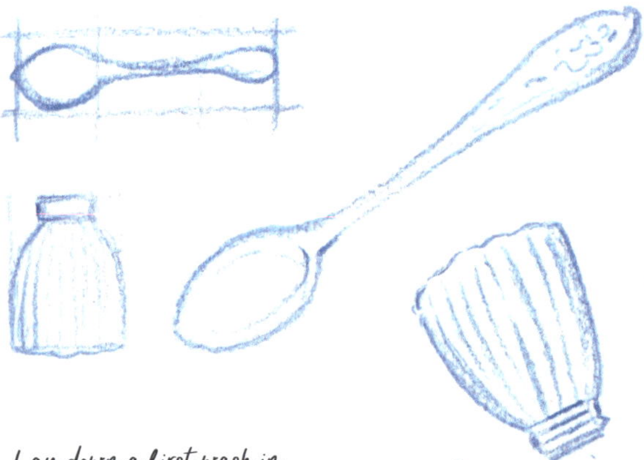

You don't need to use brown for the stems: working wet-on-wet, the red and green will merge to naturally create the stems.

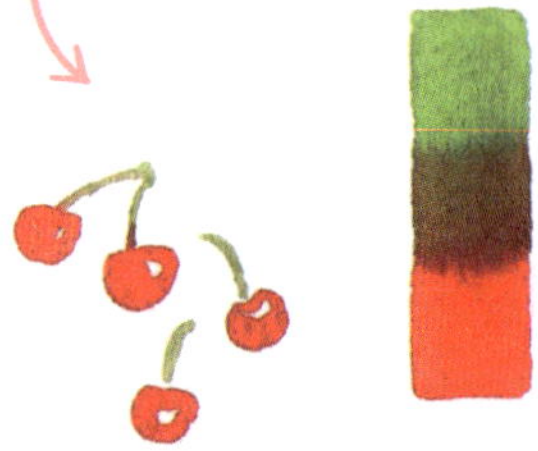

Lay down a first wash in yellow, then make a blend with a hint of vermilion red, then add alizarin red.

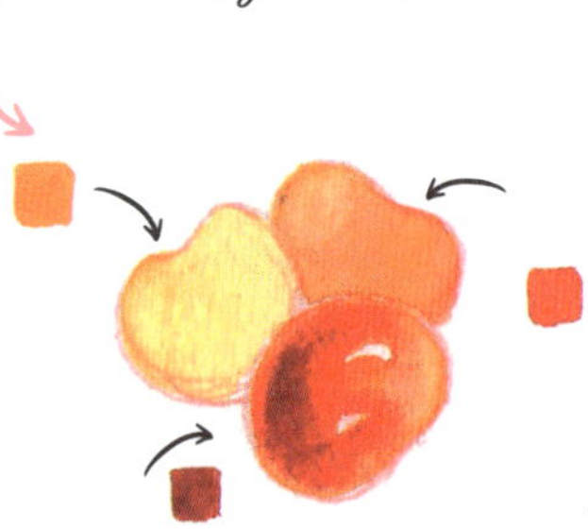

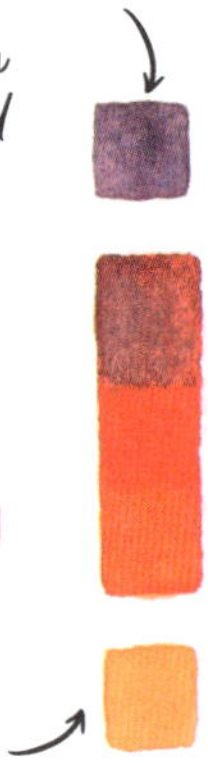

You can vary the shade of red with glazes: yellow will warm up the shadows, while purple will make them look cooler.

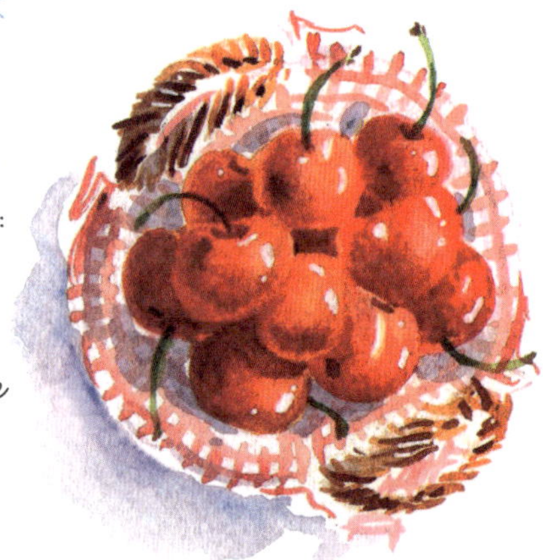

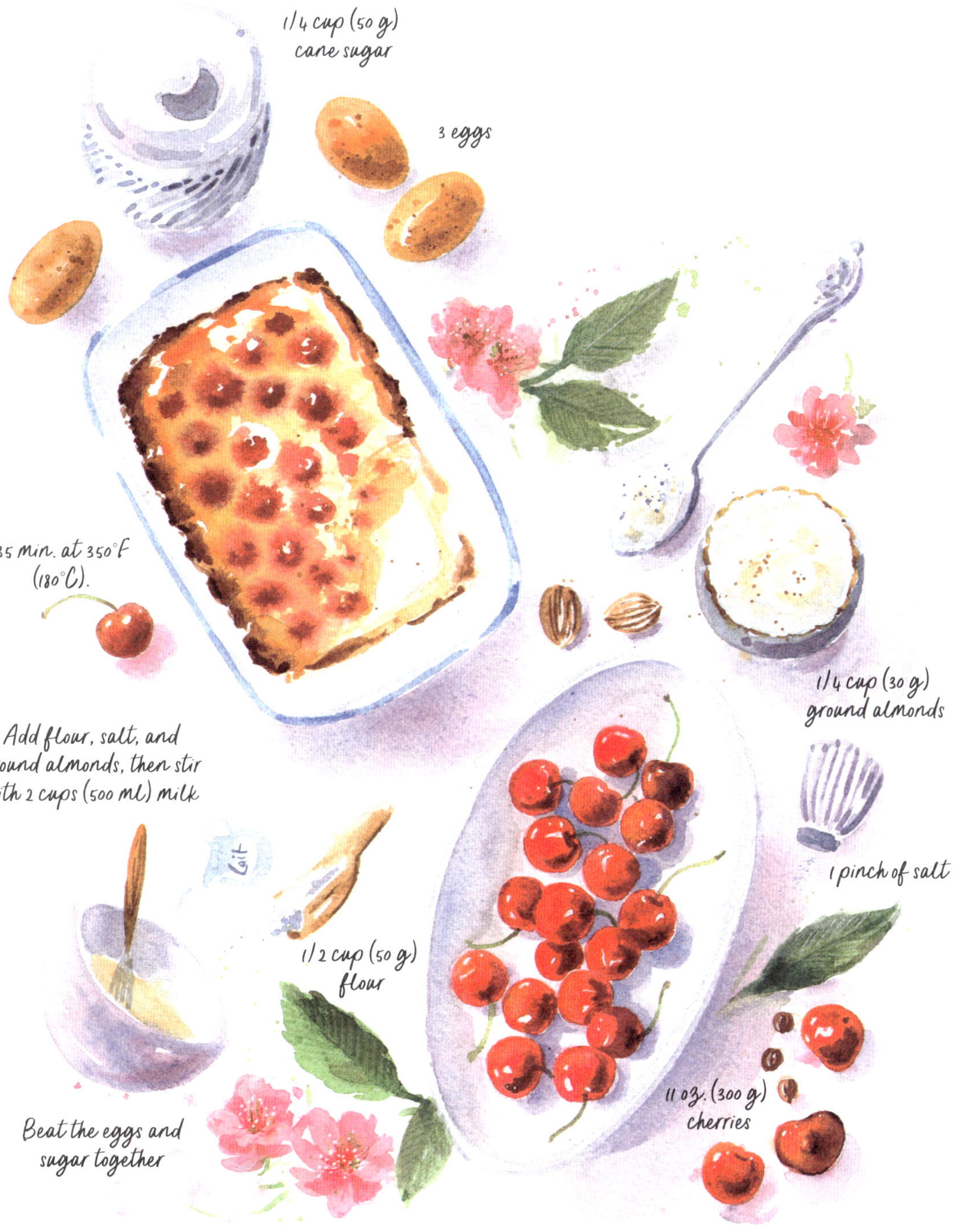
1/4 cup (50 g)
cane sugar
3 eggs
35 min. at 350°F
(180°C).
1/4 cup (30 g)
ground almonds
Add flour, salt, and
ground almonds, then stir
with 2 cups (500 ml) milk
Lait
1 pinch of salt
1/2 cup (50 g)
flour
11 oz. (300 g)
cherries
Beat the eggs and
sugar together

STRAWBERRY CHARLOTTE

Inspiration

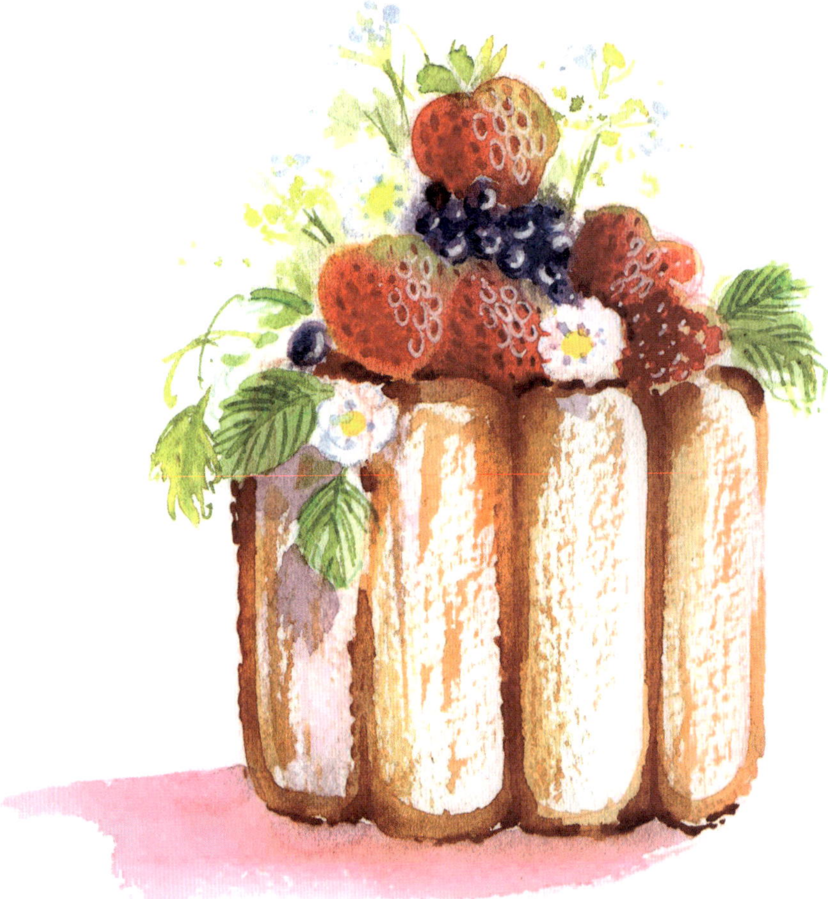

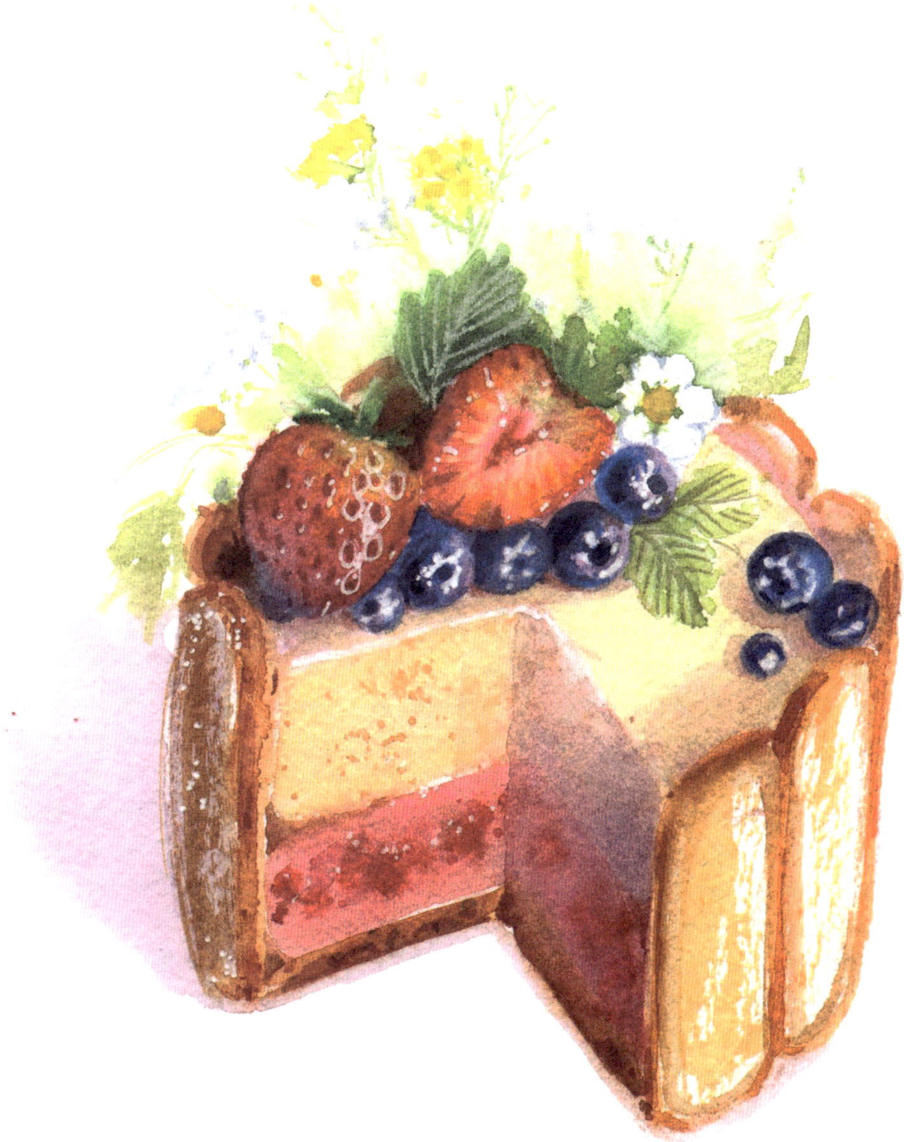

FRUIT SALAD

Recipe

Flat wash

Blends of various greens

Mix a moss green using yellow and sap green. Working wet-on-wet, make blends with a very bold green.

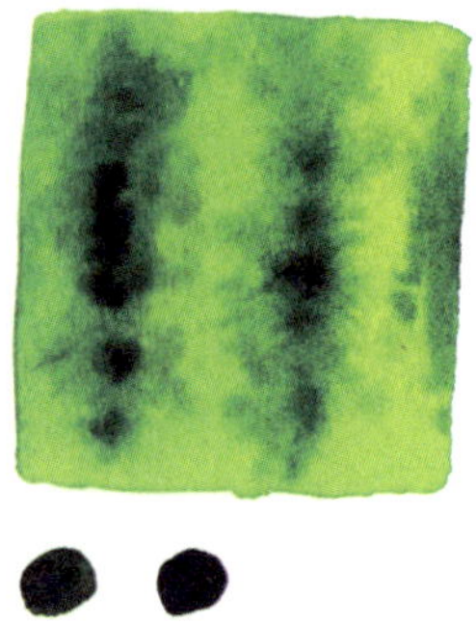

Blend a very light opera pink with permanent red light and blur the pigments afterward.

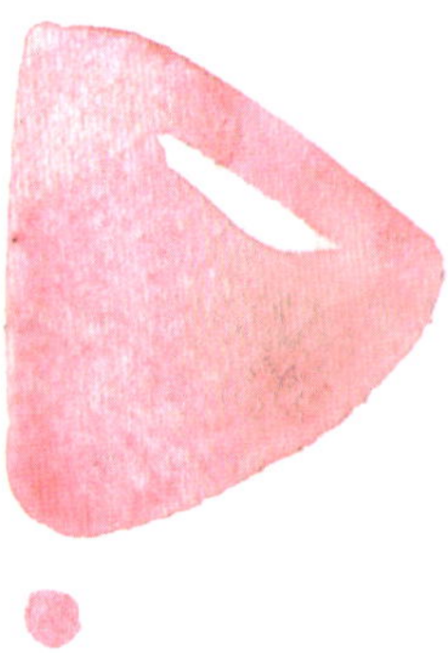

Opera pink

Permanent red light

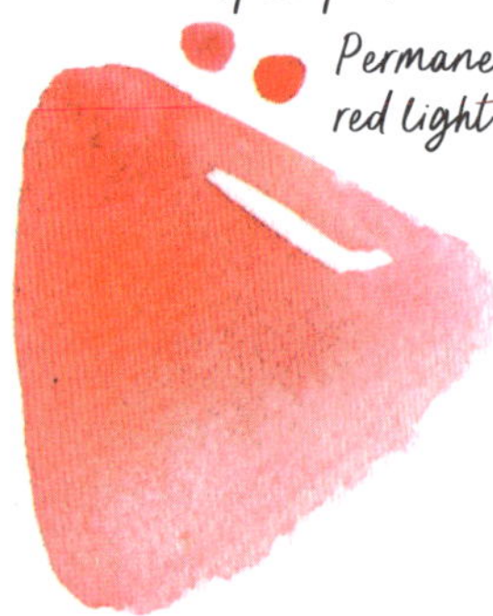

For the rind, use yellow, then a stark line of dark green on the outside.

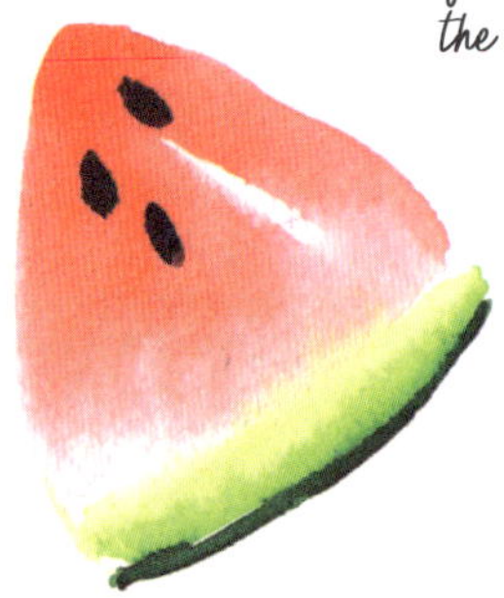

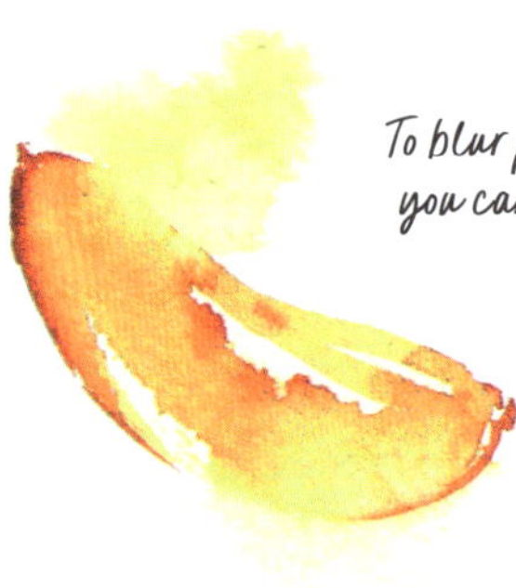

To blur part of a piece, you can spray it with water.

Yellow

Yellow + sap green

Sap green + viridian green

Payne's gray + quinacridone purple blue

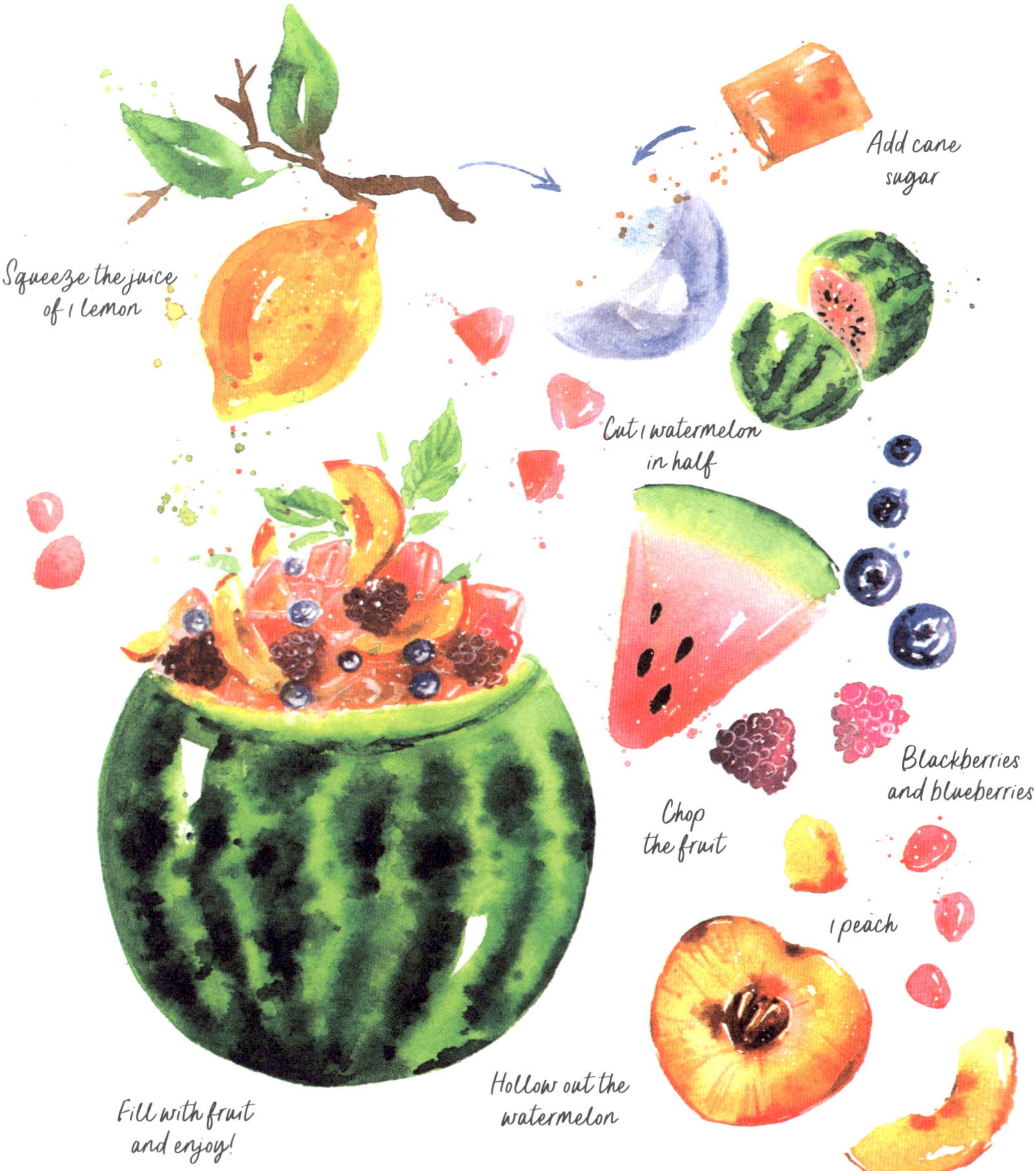
Add cane sugar
Squeeze the juice of 1 lemon
Cut 1 watermelon in half
Blackberries and blueberries
Chop the fruit
1 peach
Hollow out the watermelon
Fill with fruit and enjoy!

FRUIT JUICE

Step by Step

WATERMELON, KIWI, RASPBERRIES: WHAT GOES INTO YOUR FAVORITE FRUIT JUICE? AND WHY NOT ADD A COUPLE SMALL FLOWERS IN REFRESHING ICE CUBES TO BRIGHTEN UP THIS ASSORTMENT OF RED AND PURPLE COLORS?

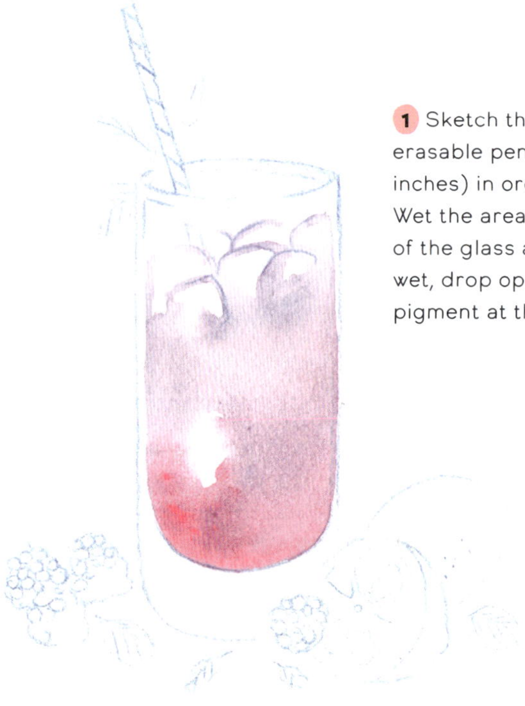

1 Sketch the glass and everything around it with an erasable pencil on a tabloid or A3 sheet (about 11 x 17 inches) in order to give your blends ample room to shine. Wet the area for the juice, taking care to avoid the edges of the glass and some of the ice cubes. Working wet-on-wet, drop opera-pink pigment at the bottom and lavender pigment at the top, letting them blend into each other.

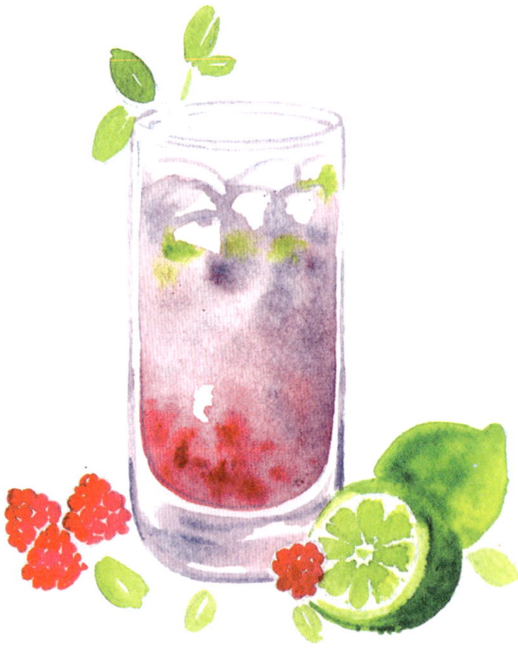

2 Drop a hint of quinacridone-rose and opera-pink pigments on the bottom of the glass as well as a few drops of moss-green pigment around the ice cubes. Paint the glass with precise, thin lines in a mauve-gray mixture. Paint the limes with blends of moss green and sap green as well as hints of viridian green. Paint the raspberries in quinacridone rose.

3 Working dry-on-dry, paint the straw and the leaves. Add green to hint at a slice of lime behind the ice cubes. Wet the background with a brush and blend in green and yellow. Bring out the raspberries with a mixture of pink and madder lake deep. Finally, highlight the reflections on the glass base with a tiny bit of cobalt blue.

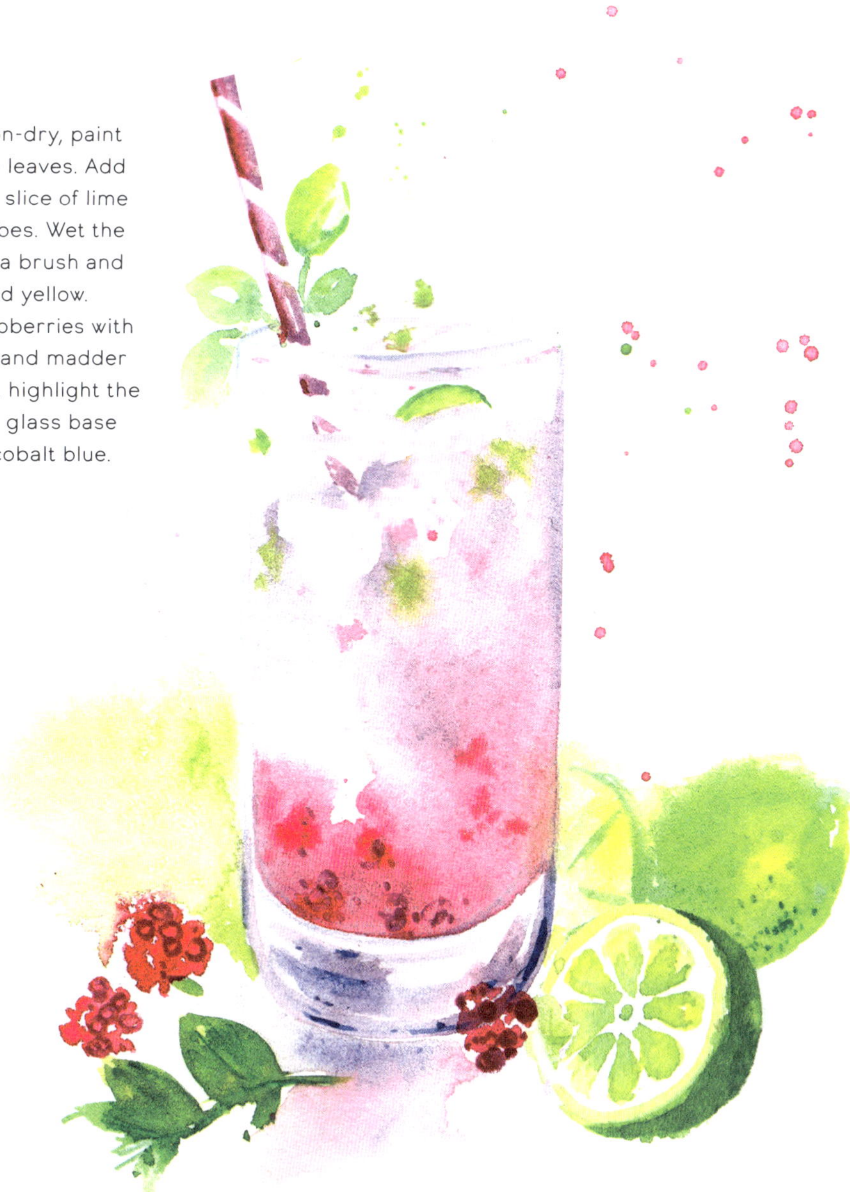

ACKNOWLEDGMENTS

To Grandaddy and Granny, to whom I owe my interest in good food and paintbrushes.

To Mom, for fostering my creative endeavors. Thank you for staying alongside me every step of the way!

To Gladys and Ludo, without whom I would not have led workshops or had the opportunity to meet so many artists!

To La Pie Curieuse, a cheerful and inspiring store and workshop that brings creations to life!

To the magnificent orchestra of life, which has always put little signs in my path to guide me and remind me to keep creating beautiful things—you always make sure that everything always works out in the end! Thank you for this beautiful enigma that enriches me every day.

Thank you, Emeline, for discovering my work; thank you for your patience and enthusiasm.

Thank you to my hands, which give me so much, and without which I would be nothing.

To my animals, the faithful, joyful companions of my sweet, solitary, and creative days.

INDEX

Note: Page numbers in *italics* indicate painting projects.

BETTER DAY BOOKS®

HAPPY • CREATIVE • CURATED

Business is personal at Better Day Books. We were founded on the belief that all people are creative and that making things by hand is inherently good for us. It's important to us that you know how much we appreciate your support. The book you are holding in your hands was crafted with the artistic passion of the author and brought to life by a team of wildly enthusiastic creatives who believed it could inspire you. If it did, please drop us a line and let us know about it. Connect with us on Instagram, post a photo of your art, and let us know what other creative pursuits you are interested in learning about. It all matters to us. You're kind of a big deal.

it's a good day to have a better day!®